# TONY KUSHNER

Tony Kushner's first play, *A Bright Room Called Day*, was produced in New York by Heat & Light Co., Inc.; and subsequently in San Francisco, Chicago, at the Bush Theatre in London, and at Joseph Papp's Public Theatre. His adaptation of Corneille's *The Illusion* has been produced at theatres around the country, including New York Theatre Workshop, Hartford Stage, the Los Angeles Theatre Center, and at Berkeley Repertory Theatre; and is currently being adapted for film for Universal Studios. Kushner also translated and adapted Goethe's *Stella* with Munich director Ulli Stephan; and co-authored, with Ariel Dorfman, the stage adaptation of Mr Dorfman's novel *Widows*, premiered at the Mark Taper Forum. *Millennium Approaches* was a winner of a 1990 Fund For New American Plays/Kennedy Center award and the 1991 Joseph Kesselring Award, and was premiered at the Eureka in the summer of 1991. Kushner is a recipient of a 1990 Whiting Foundation Writers Award, and has received playwriting fellowships from the New York State Council on the Arts and the New York Foundation for the Arts, and directing and writing grants from the National Endowment for the Arts. He has served as Director of Literary Services for Theatre Communications Group, and has taught at NYU Graduate Theatre Program, Yale University and Princeton University. He is currently playwright-in-residence at Julliard School of Drama. Kushner was born in Manhattan in 1956 and grew up in Lake Charles, Louisiana. He has a BA from Columbia University and an MFA in directing from NYU, where he studied with Carl Weber. He lives in Brooklyn.

TONY KUSHNER

# ANGELS IN AMERICA

## A Gay Fantasia on National Themes

### Part One: Millennium Approaches

ROYAL NATIONAL THEATRE

London

NICK HERN BOOKS

*Angels in America* first published in Great Britain in 1992 as a paperback original jointly by the Royal National Theatre, London and Nick Hern Books, a Random Century Company, 20 Vauxhall Bridge Road, London SW1V 2SA
Reprinted 1992

Front cover: Collage by Michael Mayhew

Lines on page 67 reproduced from *Wouldn't It Be Loverly* by permission of Warner Chappell Music

Set in Baskerville by Tek Art Ltd, Addiscombe, Croydon, Surrey
Printed by Cox & Wyman Ltd, Reading

British Library Cataloguing in Publication Data
A catalogue record for this book is available from the British Library
ISBN 1 85459 156 8

*Millennium Approaches* is for Mark Bronnenberg, my former lover, my forever friend, my safe haven and my favourite homosexual.

## Acknowledgements

I've been working on *Angels in America*, of which *Millennium Approaches* is the first part, for several years, and in the process have accumulated many debts:

I received generous support during the writing of this play in the form of grants from the National Endowment for the Arts, the Gerbode Foundation, and the Fund for New American Plays. Further financial and abundant emotional support came from my parents, Martha Deutscher, and Dot and Jerry Edelstien; Joyce Ketay the Wonder-Agent; and from Gordon Davidson and the staff of the Mark Taper Forum.

The play has benefited from the dramaturgical work of Roberta Levitow, Philip Kan Gotanda, Leon Katz, Ellen McLaughlin and David Esbjornson; and K.C. Davis contributed dramaturgy, dedication and Radical Queerness. The radiant spirit of Sigrid Wurschmidt, actress extraordinaire and angel of the world, remains a beacon light through all the darkness.

Bill Anderson, Andy Holland, Ian Kramer, Peter Minthorn, Sam Sommer and John Ryan are everywhere in this play.

Oskar Eustis's guidance, talents, intelligence and friendship have been indispensable; he called *Angels in America* into being, and without him it would never have been completed.

To Kimberly T. Flynn, for intellectual and political instruction, and for the difficult education of my heart, I owe my profoundest debts of gratitude.

## Characters

ROY M. COHN   A successful New York lawyer and unofficial power broker.

JOSEPH PORTER PITT   Chief clerk for Justice Theodore Wilson of the Federal Court of Appeals, Second Circuit.

HARPER AMATY PITT   Joe's wife, an agoraphobic with a mild valium addiction.

LOUIS IRONSON   A word processor working for the Second Circuit Court of Appeals.

PRIOR WALTER   Louis' boyfriend. Occasionally works as a club designer or caterer, mostly lives modestly off a small trust fund.

HANNAH PORTER PITT   Joe's mother, currently residing in Salt Lake City, living off her deceased husband's army pension.

BELIZE   A former drag queen and former lover of Prior's. A registered nurse. Belize's name was originally Norman Arriaga; Belize is a drag name that stuck.

THE ANGEL   Four divine emanations, Fluor, Phosphor, Lumen and Candle; manifest in One: The Continental Principality of America. She is the angel incorrectly identified by Joseph Smith as the Angel Moroni. She has magnificent pale grey wings.

## Other Characters in Part One

RABBI ISIDOR CHEMELWITZ, an orthodox Jewish rabbi, is played by the actor playing Hannah.

MR LIES, Harper's imaginary friend, a travel agent, who in style of dress and speech suggests a jazz musician; he always wears a lapel badge emblazoned with 'IOTA' (The International Order of Travel Agents). He is played by the actor playing Belize.

In Act Two, Scene Four: The man in the park is played by the actor playing Prior.

THE VOICE is the Voice of The Angel.

HENRY, Roy's doctor, is played by the actor playing Hannah.

EMILY, a nurse, is played in both Acts Two and Three by the actor playing The Angel.

MARTIN HELLER, a Reagan Administration Justice Department flackman, is played by the actor playing Harper.

ELLA CHAPTER, a Salt Lake City Real Estate Saleswoman, is played by the actor playing The Angel.

PRIOR 1, a ghost of a dead Prior Walter from the thirteenth century, is played by the actor playing Joe. He is a blunt, gloomy medieval farmer with a guttural Yorkshire accent.

PRIOR 2, a ghost of a dead Prior Walter from the eighteenth century, is played by the actor playing Roy. He is a Londoner, sophisticated, with a High British accent.

THE ESKIMO is played by the actor playing Joe.

THE WOMAN in the South Bronx is played by the actor playing The Angel.

ETHEL ROSENBERG is played by the actor playing Hannah.

**A Disclaimer:** Roy M. Cohn, the character, is based on the late Roy M. Cohn (1927–1986), who was all too real; for the most part the acts attributed to the character Roy, such as his illegal conferences with the judge in the trial of Ethel Rosenberg, are to be found in the historical record. But this Roy is a work of fiction; his words are my invention, and liberties have been taken.

**A Note About the Staging:** The play benefits from a pared-down style of presentation, with minimal scenery and scene shifts done rapidly (no blackouts!) employing the cast as well as stage-hands – which makes for an actor-driven event, as this must be. The moments of magic – the appearance and disappearance of Mr Lies and the ghosts, the Book hallucination, and the ending – are to be fully realised, as bits of wonderful *Theatrical* illusion – which means it's OK if the wires show, and maybe it's good that they do, but the magic should at the same time be thoroughly amazing.

*Angels in America Part One: Millennium Approaches* was commissioned by and received its world premiere at the Eureka Theatre Company of San Francisco. The play was further developed and produced by the Mark Taper Forum in Los Angeles.

Tony Kushner is currently developing *Part Two: Perestroika* with the Eureka Theatre company and the Mark Taper Forum. *Angels in America Parts One and Two* will receive its world premiere at the Mark Taper Forum in the 1992–3 season.

*Millennium Approaches* was first performed in a workshop production presented by Center Theatre Group/Mark Taper Forum, May 1990. It was directed by Oskar Eustis. Sets were designed by Mark Wendlend, costumes by Lydia Tanji, lights by Casey Cowan and Brian Gale, and music by Nathan Birnbaum. The cast was as follows:

| | |
|---|---|
| ROY COHN | Richard Frank |
| JOE PITT | Jeffrey King |
| HARPER PITT | Lorri Holt |
| BELIZE | Harry Waters Jr |
| LOUIS IRONSON | Jon Matthews |
| PRIOR WALTER | Stephen Spinella |
| HANNAH PITT | Kathleen Chalfant |
| THE ANGEL | Ellen McLaughlin |

The World Premiere of *Millennium Approaches* was presented by The Eureka Theatre Company, May 1991. It was directed by David Esbjornson. Sets were designed by Tom Kamm, costumes by Sandra Woodall, and lights by Jack Carpenter and Jim Cave. The cast was as follows:

| | |
|---|---|
| ROY COHN | Jon Bellucci |
| JOE PITT | Michael Scott Ryan |
| HARPER PITT | Anne Darragh |
| BELIZE | Harry Waters Jr |
| LOUIS IRONSON | Michael Ornstein |
| PRIOR WALTER | Stephen Spinella |
| HANNAH PITT | Kathleen Chalfant |
| THE ANGEL | Ellen McLaughlin |

*Angels in America* was first performed in London on the Cottesloe stage of the National Theatre. First preview was 17 January 1992 and press night 23 January 1992.

The cast, in order of speaking, was as follows:-

| | |
|---|---|
| RABBI ISIDOR CHEMELWITZ | Jeffrey Chiswick |
| ROY COHN | Henry Goodman |
| JOSEPH PORTER PITT | Nick Reding |
| HARPER AMATY PITT | Felicity Montagu |
| MR LIES | Joseph Mydell |
| LOUIS IRONSON | Marcus D'Amico |
| PRIOR WALTER | Sean Chapman |
| THE VOICE | Nancy Crane |
| HENRY, Roy's doctor | Jeffrey Chiswick |
| EMILY, a nurse | Nancy Crane |
| MAN IN THE PARK | Sean Chapman |
| BELIZE | Joseph Mydell |
| MARTIN HELLER | Jeffrey Chiswick |
| HANNAH PORTER PITT | Rosemary Martin |
| SISTER ELLA CHAPTER | Nancy Crane |
| PRIOR 1 | Nick Reding |
| PRIOR 2 | Jeffrey Chiswick |
| ESKIMO | Nick Reding |
| WOMAN IN THE SOUTH BRONX | Nancy Crane |
| ETHEL ROSENBERG | Rosemary Martin |

*Directed by* Declan Donnellan
*Designed by* Nick Ormerod
*Lighting by* Mick Hughes
*Music by* Paddy Cunneen

This text went to press before the opening night, and may therefore differ slightly from the text as performed.

## ACT ONE: BAD NEWS   Fall 1985

### Scene One

RABBI ISIDOR CHEMELWITZ *alone onstage with a small coffin. It is a rough pine box with two wooden pegs, one at the foot and one at the head, holding the lid in place. A prayer, shawl emboidered with a Star of David is draped over the lid, and by the head a yarzheit candle is burning.*

RABBI ISIDOR CHEMELWITZ *(he speaks sonorously, with a heavy Eastern European accent, unapologetically consulting a sheet of notes for the family name.)* Hello and good morning. I am Rabbi Isidor Chemelwitz of the Bronx Home for Aged Hebrews. We are here this morning to pay respects at the passing of Sarah Ironson, devoted wife of Benjamin Ironson, also deceased, loving and caring mother of her sons Morris, Abraham, and Samuel, and her daughters Esther and Rachel; beloved grandmother of Max, Mark, Louis, Lisa, Maria . . . uh . . . Lesley, Angela, Luke and Eric. *(Looks closer at paper.)* Eric? *(Shrugs.)* Eric. A large and loving family. We assemble that we may mourn collectively this good and righteous woman.

*He looks at the coffin*

This woman. I did not know this woman. I cannot accurately describe her attributes, nor do justice to her dimensions. She was . . . Well, in the Bronx Home of Aged Hebrews are many like this, the old, and to many I speak but not, to be frank, with this one. She preferred silence. So I do not know her and yet I know her. We are all the same, of this generation. We are the last of our kind.

*He touches the coffin.*

In her was – not a person but a whole kind of person – the ones who crossed the ocean, who brought with us to America the villages of Russia and Lithuania – and how we struggled, and how we fought, for the family, for the Jewish home, so that you would not grow up *here*, in this strange place, in the melting pot where nothing melted. Descendants of this

immigrant woman, you do not grow up in America, you and
your children and their children with the goyische names, you
do not live in America, no such place exists, your clay is the
clay of some Litvak shtetl, your air the air of the steppes –
because she carried the old world on her back across the ocean,
in a boat, and she put it down on Grand Concourse Avenue, or
in Flatbush, and she worked that earth into your bones, and
you pass it to your children, this ancient, ancient culture and
home.

*Little pause.*

You can never make that crossing that she made, for such
Great Voyages in this world do not any more exist. But every
day of your lives the miles that voyage between that place and
this one you cross. Every day. You understand me? In you that
journey is.
So . . .
She was the last of the Mohicans, this one was. Pretty soon . . .
all the old will be dead.

**Scene Two**

ROY *and* JOE *in* ROY's *office.* ROY *at an impressive desk, bare except
for a very elaborate phone system, rows and rows of flashing buttons
which bleep and beep and whistle incessantly, making chaotic music
underneath* ROY's *conversations.* JOE *is waiting.* ROY *conducts
business with great energy, impatience, and sensual abandon:
gesticulating, shouting, cajoling, crooning, playing the phone, receiver
and hold button with virtuosity and love.*

ROY (*hitting a button*). Hold. (*To* JOE.) I wish I was an octopus, a
    fucking octopus. Eight loving arms and all those suckers. Know
    what I mean?

JOE. No, I . . .

ROY (*gesturing to a deli platter of little sandwiches on his desk*). You
    want lunch?

JOE. No, that's OK really I just . . .

ROY (*hitting a button*). Ailene? Roy Cohn. Now what kind of a
    greeting is . . . I thought we were friends, Ai . . . Look Mrs

Soffer you don't have to get . . . You're upset. You're yelling.
You'll aggravate your condition, you shouldn't yell, you'll pop
little blood vessels in your face if you yell – No that was a joke,
Mrs Soffer, I was joking . . . I already apologised sixteen times
for that, Mrs Soffer, you . . . (*While she's fulminating,* ROY *covers
the mouthpiece with his hand and talks to* JOE.) This'll take a
minute, *eat* already, what is this tasty sandwich here it's (*He takes
a bite of a sandwich.*) Mmmmm, liver or some . . . Here.

*He pitches the sandwich to* JOE, *who catches it and returns it to the
platter.*

ROY (*back to* MRS SOFFER). Uh huh, uh huh . . . No, I already
told you it wasn't a vacation it was business, Mrs Soffer, I have
clients in Haiti, Mrs Soffer, I . . . Listen, Ailene, YOU THINK
I'M THE ONLY GODDAMN LAWYER IN HISTORY EVER
MISSED A COURT DATE? Don't make such a big fucking . . .
Hold. (*He hits the hold button.*) You HAG!

JOE. If this is a bad time . . .

ROY. *Bad* time? This is a *good* time! (*Button.*) Baby doll, get
me . . . Oh fuck, wait . . . (*Button, button.*) Hello? Yah. Sorry to
keep you holding, Judge Hollins, I . . . Oh *Mrs* Hollins, sorry
dear deep voice you got. Enjoying your visit? (*Hand over
mouthpiece again, to* JOE.) She sounds like a truck driver and he
sounds like Kate Smith, very confusing, Nixon appointed him,
all the geeks are Nixon appointees . . . (*To* MRS HOLLINS.)
Yeah, yeah right good so how many tickets dear? Seven. For
what, *Cats, Forty-Second Street,* what? No you wouldn't like *La
Cage,* trust me, I know. Oh for godsake . . . Hold. (*Button,
button.*) Baby doll, seven for *Cats* or something, anything hard
to get, I don't give a fuck what and neither will they. (*Button; to*
JOE.) You see *La Cage*?

JOE. No, I . . .

ROY. Fabulous. Best thing on Broadway. Maybe ever. (*Button.*)
Who? Aw, Jesus H. Christ, Harry, *no,* Harry, Judge John
Francis Grimes, Manhattan Family Court. Do I have to do
every goddam thing myself? *Touch* the bastard, Harry, and
don't call me on this line again, I told you not to . . .

JOE. Roy, uh, should I wait outside or . . .

ROY (*to* JOE). Oh sit. (*To* HARRY.) You hold. I pay you to hold
fuck you Harry you jerk. (*Button.*) Half-wit dick-brain. (*Instantly*

*philosophical*.) I see the universe, Joe, as a kind of sandstorm in outerspace with winds of mega-hurricane velocity but instead of grains of sand it's.shards and splinters of glass. You ever feel that way? Ever have one of those days?

JOE. I'm not sure I . . .

ROY. So how's life in Appeals? How's the Judge?

JOE. He sends his best.

ROY. He's a good man. Loyal. Not the brightest man on the bench, but he has manners. And a nice head of silver hair.

JOE. He gives me a lot of responsibility.

ROY. Yeah, like writing his decisions and signing his name.

JOE. Well . . .

ROY. He's a nice guy. And you cover admirably.

JOE. Well, thanks, Roy, I . . .

ROY (*button*). Yah? Who is *this*? Well who the fuck are *you*? Hold – (*Button*.) Mrs Soffer? Feeling better Mrs Soffer? Well, you *have* to hold, it's crazy busy here, I . . . I *like* the music, Sinatra, everyone likes holding to Sinatra . . . Yes. Taken care of. Yes. What? Do I *what*? (*Little pause;* ROY *puts receiver against forehead, sighs, looks at* JOE *and rolls his eyes, then*.) What do you mean do I know the judge, Mrs Soffer? That's illegal, Mrs Soffer. No, no I do not know the judge, I . . . hold . . . (*Button; under his breath*.) Of course I know the fucking judge you dumb bitch. (*Button*.) Harry? Eighty-seven grand, something like that. Fuck him. Eat me. New Jersey, chain of porno film stores in, uh, Weehawken. That's – Harry, that's the beauty of the law. (*Button*.) So, Baby doll, what? *Cats*? Ugh. (*Button*.) *Cats!* It's about cats. Singing cats, you'll love it. Eight o'clock, the theatre's always at eight. (*Button*.) Fucking tourists. (*Button, then to* JOE.) Oh live a little, Joe, *eat* something for Christ sake –

JOE. Um, Roy, could you . . .

ROY. What? (*To* HARRY.)
Hold a minute. (*Button*.)
Mrs . . . (*Button*.) God-
fucking-dammit to hell,
where is . . . well she was
here a minute ago, baby doll,
see if . . .

JOE. Roy, I'd really appreciate
  it if . . .

*The phone starts making three different beeping sounds, all at once.*

ROY (*smashing buttons*). Jesus
  fuck this goddam thing . . .          JOE. I really wish you
  Baby doll? Ring the Post get            wouldn't . . .
  me Suzy see if . . .

*The phone starts whistling loudly.*

ROY. CHRIST!

JOE. *Roy.*

ROY (*into receiver.*) Hold. (*Button; to* JOE.) *What?*

JOE. Could you please not take the Lord's name in vain?

*Pause.*

JOE. I'm sorry. But please. At least while I'm . . .

ROY (*laughs, then*). Right. Sorry. Fuck. Only in America. (*Punches a button.*) Baby doll, tell 'em all to fuck off. Tell 'em I died. You handle Mrs Soffer. I'll call her back. I *will* call her. I *know* how much I borrowed. She's got four hundred times that stuffed up her . . . yeah, tell her I said that. (*Button. The phone is silent.*) So, Joe.

JOE. I'm sorry Roy, I just . . .

ROY. No no no no, principles count, I respect principles. I'm not religious but I like God and God likes me. Baptist, Catholic?

JOE. Mormon.

ROY. Mormon. Delectable. Absolutely. Only in America. So, Joe. Whattya think?

JOE. It's . . . well . . .

ROY. Crazy life.

JOE. Chaotic.

ROY. Well but God bless chaos. Right?

JOE. Ummm . . .

ROY. Huh. Mormons. I knew Mormons, in, um, Nevada.

JOE. Utah, mostly.

ROY. No, these Mormons were in Vegas.
  So. So, how'd you like to go to Washington and work for the Justice Department?

JOE. Sorry?

ROY. How'd you like to go to Washington and work for the
Justice Department? All I gotta do is pick up the phone, talk to
Ed, and you're in.

JOE. In . . . what, exactly?

ROY. Associate Assistant Something Big. Internal Affairs, heart
of the woods, something nice with clout.

JOE. Ed . . .?

ROY. The Attorney General.

JOE. Oh.

ROY. I just have to pick up the phone . . .

JOE. I have to think.

ROY. Of course.

*Pause.*

It's a great time to be in Washington, Joe.

JOE. Roy, it's incredibly exciting . . .

ROY. And it would mean something to me. You understand?

*Little pause.*

JOE. I . . . can't say how much I appreciate this Roy, I'm sort
of . . . well, stunned, I mean . . . Thanks, Roy. But I have to
give it some thought. I have to ask my wife.

ROY. Your wife. Of course.

JOE. But I really appreciate . . .

ROY. Of course. Talk to your wife.


**Scene Three**

*Split scene:* HARPER *at home alone, and* RABBI CHEMELWITZ *at
the funeral home. At first, all we see is* HARPER. *She is listening to the
radio and talking to herself, as she often does. She speaks to the audience.*

HARPER. People who are lonely, people left alone, sit talking
nonsense to the air, imagining . . . beautiful systems dying, old
fixed orders spiralling apart . . .

When you look at the ozone layer, from outside, from a
spaceship, it looks like a pale blue halo, a gentle, shimmering
aureole encircling the atmosphere encircling the earth. Thirty
miles above our heads, a thin layer of three-atom oxygen
molecules, product of photosynthesis, which explains the fussy
vegetable preference for visible light, its rejection of darker
rays and emanations. Danger from without.

It's a kind of gift, from God, the crowning touch to the
creation of the world: guardian angels, hands linked, make a
spherical net, a blue-green nesting orb, a shell of safety for life
itself. But everywhere, things are collapsing, lies surfacing,
systems of defence giving way . . . This is why, Joe, this is why I
shouldn't be left alone. (*Little pause.*)

I'd like to go travelling . . . Leave you behind to worry. I'll
send postcards with strange stamps and tantalising messages on
the back. 'Later maybe.' 'Nevermore . . .'

MR LIES, *a travel agent appears.*

HARPER. Oh! You startled me!

MR LIES. Cash, cheque or credit card?

HARPER. I remember you. You're from Salt Lake. You sold us
the plane tickets when we flew here. What are you doing in
Brooklyn?

MR LIES. You said you wanted to travel . . .

HARPER. And here you are. How thoughtful.

MR LIES. Mr Lies. Of the International Order of Travel Agents.
We mobilise the globe, we set people adrift, we stir the
populace and send nomads eddying across the planet. We are
adepts of motion, acolytes of the flux. Cash, cheque or credit
card. Name your destination.

HARPER. Antarctica, maybe. I want to see the hole in the ozone.
I heard on the radio . . .

MR LIES (*He has a computer terminal in his briefcase*). I can arrange
a guided tour. Now?

HARPER. Soon. Maybe soon. I'm not safe here you see. Things
aren't right with me. Weird stuff happens . . .

MR LIES. Like?

HARPER. Well, like you, for instance. Just appearing. Or last
week . . . well never mind.

People are like planets, you need a thick skin. Things get to me, Joe stays away and now . . . Well look. My dreams are talking back to me.

MR LIES. It's the price of rootlessness. Motion sickness. The only cure: To keep moving.

*The* RABBI *and the coffin become visible, to the audience but not to* HARPER. *The* RABBI *puts his hand on the coffin and, as if singing to the person inside, begins to intone the Kaddish.* HARPER'*s speech following the Kaddish is spoken over the prayer. Perhaps the Kaddish comes through her radio.*

RABBI ISIDOR CHEMELWITZ. Yisgadal ve'yiskadash sh'mey rabo, b'olmo deevro chiroosey ve'yamlich malchusey, bechayeychon uv'yomechechon uvchayey d'chol beys yisroel, ba'agolo uvizman koriv, ve'imroo omain. Yehey sh'mey rabo m'vorach l'olam ulolmey olmayoh. Yisborach ve'yishtabach ve'yispoar ve'yisroman ve'yisnasey ve'yis'hadar ve'yisalleh ve'yishallol sh'mey dekudsho berich hoo le'eylo min kol birchoso veshiroso, tushbchoso venechemoso, daameeron b'olmo ve'imroo omain. Y'he sh'lomo rabbo min sh'mayo v'chayim olenu v'al kol yisroel, v'imru omain. Oseh sholom bimromov, hu ya-aseh sholom olenu v'al col yisroel, v'imru omain.

HARPER (*over the Kaddish*). I'm undecided. I feel . . . that something's going to give. It's fifteen years till the second millennium. Maybe Christ will come again. Maybe seeds will be planted, maybe there'll be harvests then, maybe early figs to eat, maybe new life, maybe fresh blood, maybe companionship and love and protection, safety from what's outside, maybe the door will hold, or maybe . . . maybe the troubles will come, and the end will come, and the sky will collapse and there will be terrible rains and showers of poison light, or maybe my life is really fine, maybe Joe loves me and I'm only crazy thinking otherwise, or maybe not, maybe it's even worse than I know, maybe . . . I want to know, maybe I don't. The suspense, Mr Lies, it's killing me.

MR LIES. I suggest a vacation.

HARPER (*hearing something*). That was the elevator. Oh God; I should fix myself up, I . . . You have to go, you shouldn't be here . . . you aren't even real.

MR LIES. Call me when you decide . . .

HARPER. Go!

*The* TRAVEL AGENT *vanishes and the* RABBI *fades away, as* JOE *enters.*

JOE. Buddy?
Buddy? Sorry I'm late. I was just . . . out. Walking.
Are you mad?

HARPER. I got a little anxious.

JOE. Buddy kiss.

*They kiss.*

JOE. Nothing to get anxious about.
So. So how'd you like to move to Washington?


**Scene Four**

LOUIS *and* PRIOR *outside the funeral home, sitting on a bench, both dressed in funereal finery, talking. The funeral service for Sarah Ironson has just concluded and* LOUIS *is about to leave for the cemetery.*

LOUIS. My grandmother actually saw Emma Goldman speak. In Yiddish. But all Grandma could remember was that she spoke well and wore a hat.
What a weird service. That rabbi . . .

PRIOR. A definite find. Get his number when you go to the graveyard. I want him to bury me.

LOUIS. Better head out there. Everyone gets to put dirt on the coffin once it's lowered in.

PRIOR. Oooh. Cemetery fun. Don't want to miss that.

LOUIS. It's an old Jewish custom to express love. Here, Grandma, have a shovelful. Latecomers run the risk of finding the grave completely filled.
She was pretty crazy. She was up there in that home for ten years, talking to herself. I never visited. She looked too much like my mother.

PRIOR (*hugs him*). Poor Louis. I'm sorry your grandma is dead.

LOUIS. Tiny little coffin, huh?

Sorry I didn't introduce you to . . . I always get so closety at these family things.

PRIOR. Butch. You get butch. (*Imitating*.) 'Hi Cousin Doris, you don't remember me I'm Lou, Rachel's boy.' Lou, not Louis, because if you say Louis they'll hear the sibillant S.

LOUIS. I don't have a . . .

PRIOR. I don't blame you, hiding. Bloodlines. Jewish curses are the worst. I personally would dissolve if anyone ever looked me in the eye and said 'Feh.' Fortunately WASPS don't say 'Feh.' Oh and by the way, darling, cousin Doris is a dyke.

LOUIS. No.
Really?

PRIOR. You don't notice *anything*. If I hadn't spent the last four years fellating you I'd swear you were straight.

LOUIS. You're in a pissy mood. Cat still missing?

*Little pause.*

PRIOR. Not a furball in sight. It's your fault.

LOUIS. It is?

PRIOR. I warned you, Louis. Names are important. Call an animal 'Little Sheba' and you can't expect it to stick around. Besides, it's a dog's name.

LOUIS. I wanted a dog in the first place, not a cat. He sprayed my books.

PRIOR. He was a female cat.

LOUIS. Cats are stupid, high-strung predators. Babylonians sealed them up in bricks. Dogs have brains.

PRIOR. Cats have intuition.

LOUIS. A sharp dog is as smart as a really dull two-year-old child.

PRIOR. Cats know when something's wrong.

LOUIS. Only if you stop feeding them.

PRIOR. They know. That's why Sheba left, because she knew.

LOUIS. Knew what?

*Pause.*

PRIOR. I did my best Shirley Booth this morning, floppy slippers, housecoat, curlers, can of Little Friskies; 'Come back, Little Sheba, come back . . .' To no avail. Le chat, elle ne reviendra jamais, jamais . . .

*He removes his jacket, rolls up his sleeve, shows* LOUIS *a dark-purple spot on the underside of his arm near the shoulder.*

See.

LOUIS. That's just a burst blood vessel.

PRIOR. Not according to the best medical authorities.

LOUIS. What?

*Pause.*

Tell me.

PRIOR. K.S. baby. Lesion number one. Lookit. The wine-dark kiss of the angel of death.

LOUIS (*very softly, holding* PRIOR's *arm*). Oh please . . .

PRIOR. I'm a lesionnaire. The Foreign Lesion. The American Lesion. Lesionnaire's disease.

LOUIS. Stop.

PRIOR. My troubles are lesion.

LOUIS. Will you *stop.*

PRIOR. Don't you think I'm handling this well?
    I'm going to die.

LOUIS. Bullshit.

PRIOR. Let go of my arm.

LOUIS. No.

PRIOR. Let go.

LOUIS (*grabbing* PRIOR, *embracing him ferociously*). No.

PRIOR. I can't find a way to spare you baby.
    No wall like the wall of hard scientific fact. K.S. Wham. Bang your head on that.

LOUIS. Fuck you. (*Letting go.*) Fuck you fuck you fuck you.

PRIOR. Now that's what I like to hear. A mature reaction.
    Let's go see if the cat's come home.
    Louis?

LOUIS. When did you find this?

PRIOR. I couldn't tell you.

LOUIS. Why?

PRIOR. I was scared, Lou.

LOUIS. Of what?

PRIOR. That you'll leave me.

LOUIS. Oh.

*Little pause.*

PRIOR. Bad timing, funeral and all, but I figured as long as we're on the subject of death . . .

LOUIS. I have to go bury my grandma.

PRIOR. Lou?

*Pause.*

Then you'll come home?

LOUIS. Then I'll come home.


**Scene Five**

*Split scene:* JOE *and* HARPER *at home;* LOUIS *at the cemetery with* RABBI ISIDOR CHEMELWITZ *and the little coffin.*

HARPER. Washington?

JOE. It's an incredible honour, buddy, and . . .

HARPER. I have to think.

JOE. Of course.

HARPER. Say no.

JOE. You said you were going to think about it.

HARPER. I don't want to move to Washington.

JOE. Well I do.

HARPER. It's a giant cemetery, huge white graves and mausoleums everywhere.

JOE. We could live in Maryland. Or Georgetown.

HARPER. We're happy here.

JOE. That's not really true, buddy, we . . .

HARPER. Well happy enough! Pretend-happy. That's better than nothing.

JOE. It's time to make some changes, Harper.

HARPER. No changes. Why?

JOE. I've been chief clerk for four years. I make twenty-nine thousand dollars a year. That's ridiculous. I graduated fourth in my class and I make less than anyone I know. And I'm . . . I'm tired of being a clerk, I want to go where something good is happening

HARPER. Nothing good happens in Washington. We'll forget church teachings and buy furniture at . . . at *Conran's* and become yuppies. I have too much to do here.

JOE. Like what?

HARPER. I *do* have things . . .

JOE. What things?

HARPER. I have to finish painting the bedroom.

JOE. You've been painting in there for over a year.

HARPER. I know, I . . . It just isn't done because I never get time to finish it.

JOE. Oh that's . . . that doesn't make sense. You have all the time in the world. You could finish it when I'm at work.

HARPER. I'm afraid to go in there alone.

JOE. Afraid of what?

HARPER. I heard someone in there. Metal scraping on the wall. A man with a knife, maybe.

JOE. There's no one in the bedroom, Harper.

HARPER. Not now.

JOE. Not this morning either.

HARPER. How do you know? You were at work this morning. There's something creepy about this place. Remember *Rosemary's Baby*?

JOE. *Rosemary's Baby?*

HARPER. Our apartment looks like that one. Wasn't that apartment in Brooklyn?

JOE. No, it was . . .

HARPER. Well, it looked like this. It did.

JOE. Then let's move.

HARPER. Georgetown's worse. *The Exorcist* was in Georgetown.

JOE. The devil, everywhere you turn, huh, buddy.

HARPER. Yeah. Everywhere.

JOE. How many pills today, buddy?

HARPER. None. One. Three. Only three.

LOUIS (*pointing at the coffin*). Why are there just two little wooden pegs holding the lid down?

RABBI ISIDOR CHEMELWITZ. So she can get out easier if she wants to.

LOUIS. I hope she stays put.
   I pretended for years that she was already dead. When they called to say she had died it was a surprise. I abandoned her.

RABBI ISIDOR CHEMELWITZ. 'Sharfer vi di tson fun a shlang iz an umbedankbar kind!'

LOUIS. I don't speak Yiddish.

RABBI ISIDOR CHEMELWITZ. Sharper than the serpent's tooth is the ingratitude of children. Shakespeare. 'Kenig Lear.'

LOUIS. Rabbi, what does the Holy Writ say about someone who abandons someone he loves at a time of great need?

RABBI ISIDOR CHEMELWITZ. Why would a person do such a thing?

LOUIS. Because he has to.
   Maybe because this person's sense of the world, that it will change for the better with struggle, maybe a person who has this neo-Hegelian positivist sense of constant historical progress towards happiness or perfection or something, who feels very powerful because he feels connected to these forces, moving uphill all the time . . . maybe that person can't, um, incorporate

sickness into his sense of how things are supposed to go. Maybe vomit . . . and sores and disease . . . really frighten him, maybe . . . he isn't so good with death.

RABBI ISIDOR CHEMELWITZ. The Holy Scriptures have nothing to say about such a person.

LOUIS. Rabbi, I'm afraid of the crimes I may commit.

RABBI ISIDOR CHEMELWITZ. Please, mister. I'm a sick old rabbi facing a long drive home to the Bronx. You want to confess, better you should find a priest.

LOUIS. But I'm not a Catholic, I'm a Jew.

RABBI ISIDOR CHEMELWITZ. Worse luck for you, bubbulah. Catholics believe in forgiveness. Jews believe in Guilt. (*He pats the coffin tenderly.*)

LOUIS. You just make sure those pegs are in good and tight.

RABBI ISIDOR CHEMELWITZ. Don't worry, minster. The life she had, she'll stay put. She's better off.

JOE. Look, I know this is scary for you. But try to understand what it means to me. Will you try?

HARPER. Yes.

JOE. Good. Really try.
    I think things are starting to change in the world.

HARPER. But I don't want . . .

JOE: Wait. For the good. Change for the good. America has rediscovered itself. Its sacred position among nations. And people aren't ashamed of that like they used to be. This is a great thing. The truth restored. Law restored. That's what President Reagan's done, Harper. He says 'Truth exists and can be spoken proudly.' And the country responds to him. We become better. More good. I need to be a part of that, I need something big to lift me up. I mean, six years ago the world seemed in decline, horrible, hopeless, full of unsolvable problems and crime and confusion and hunger and . . .

HARPER. But it still seems that way. More now than before. They say the ozone layer is . . .

JOE. Harper . . .

HARPER. And today out of the window on Atlantic Avenue there was a schizophrenic traffic cop who was making these . . .

JOE. Stop it! I'm trying to make a point.

HARPER. So am I.

JOE. You aren't even making sense, you . . .

HARPER. My point is the world seems just as . . .

JOE. It only seems that way to you because you never go out in the world, Harper, and you have emotional problems.

HARPER. I do so get out in the world.

JOE. You don't. You stay in all day, fretting about imaginary . . .

HARPER. I get out. I do. You don't know what I do.

JOE. You don't stay in all day.

HARPER. No.

JOE. Well . . . Yes you do.

HARPER. That's what you think.

JOE. Where do you go?

HARPER. Where do *you* go? When you walk. (*Pause, then angrily.*) And I DO NOT have emotional problems.

JOE. I'm sorry.

HARPER. And If I do have emotional problems it's from living with you. Or . . .

JOE. I'm sorry buddy, I didn't mean to . . .

HARPER. Or if you do think I do then you should never have married me. You have all these secrets and lies.

JOE. I want to be married to you, Harper.

HARPER. You shouldn't. You never should.

*Pause.*

Hey buddy. Hey buddy.

JOE. Buddy kiss . . .

*They kiss.*

HARPER. I heard on the radio how to give a blowjob.

JOE. What?

HARPER. You want to try?

JOE. You really shouldn't listen to stuff like that.

HARPER. Mormons can give blowjobs.

JOE. *Harper.*

HARPER (*imitating his tone*). *Joe.*
   It was a little Jewish lady with a German accent.
      This is a good time. For me to make a baby.
      Then they went on to a programme about holes in the ozone
   layer. Over Antarctica. Skin burns, birds go blind, icebergs
   melt. The world's coming to an end.


**Scene Six**

*In the men's room of the offices of the Brooklyn Federal Courts Of
Appeals; the last word in legal/corporate lavatory; LOUIS is crying over
the sink; JOE enters.*

JOE. Oh, um . . . Morning.

LOUIS. Good morning, counsellor.

JOE (*he watches* LOUIS *cry*). Sorry, I . . . I don't know your name.

LOUIS. Don't bother. Word processor. The lowest of the low.

JOE (*holding out his hand*). Joe Pitt. I'm with Justice Wilson . . .

LOUIS. Oh, I know that. Counsellor Pitt. Chief Clerk.

JOE. Were you . . . are you OK?

LOUIS. Oh, yeah. Thanks. What a nice man.

JOE. Not so nice.

LOUIS. What?

JOE. Not so nice. Nothing. You sure you're . . .

LOUIS. Life sucks shit. Life . . . just sucks shit.

JOE. What's wrong?

LOUIS. Run in my nylons.

JOE. Sorry . . .?

LOUIS. Forget it. Look, thanks for asking.

JOE. Well . . .

LOUIS. I mean it really is nice of you.

*He starts crying again.*

Sorry, sorry, sick friend . . .

JOE. Oh, I'm sorry.

LOUIS. Yeah, yeah, well, that's sweet.
Three of your colleagues have preceded you to this baleful sight and you're the first one to ask. The others just opened the door, saw me, and fled. I hope they had to pee real bad.

JOE (*handing him a wad of toilet paper*). They just didn't want to intrude.

LOUIS. Hah. Reaganite heartless macho asshole lawyers.

JOE. Oh, that's unfair.

LOUIS. What is? Heartless? Macho? Reaganite? Lawyer?

JOE. I voted for Reagan.

LOUIS. You did?

JOE. Twice.

LOUIS. Twice? Well, oh boy. A Gay Republican.

JOE. Excuse me?

LOUIS. Nothing.

JOE. I'm not . . .
Forget it.

LOUIS. Republican? Not Republican? Or . . .

JOE. What?

LOUIS. What?

JOE. Not gay. I'm not gay.

LOUIS. Oh. Sorry.
(*Blows his nose loudly.*) It's just . . .

JOE. Yes?

LOUIS. Well, sometimes you can tell from the way a person
sounds, that . . . I mean you *sound* like a . . .

JOE. No I don't. Like what?

LOUIS. Like a Republican.

*Little pause. JOE makes sure no one else is around, then.*

JOE. Do I? Sound like a . . .?

LOUIS. What? Like a . . .? Republican, or . . .? Do *I*?

JOE. Do you what?

LOUIS. Sound like a . . .?

JOE. Like a . . .?
What are we talking about? I'm . . . confused.

LOUIS. Yes.
My name is Louis. But all my friends call me Louise. I work
in Word Processing. Thanks for the toilet paper.

LOUIS *offers* JOE *his hand,* JOE *reaches,* LOUIS *feints and pecks*
JOE *on the cheek, and exits.*


**Scene Seven**

*Mutual dream scene.* PRIOR *is at the make-up table, applying the face.*
HARPER *is having a pill-induced hallucination. She has these from*
*time to time. For some reason,* PRIOR *has appeared in this one.*

PRIOR. (*putting on make-up, then examining the results in the mirror;*
*to the audience*). 'I'm ready for my close-up, Mr DeMille.'
One wants to move through life with elegance and grace,
blossoming infrequently but with exquisite taste, and perfect
timing, like a rare bloom, a zebra orchid . . . One wants . . . But
one so seldom gets what one wants, does one? No. One does
not. One gets fucked. Over. One . . . dies at thirty, robbed
of . . . decades of majesty . . . Fuck. This. Shit. Fuck. This. Shit.

*He studies his handiwork.*

I look like a corpse. A corpsette. Oh my queen; you know
you've hit rock-bottom when even drag is a drag.

HARPER *appears.*

HARPER. Are you . . . Who are you?

PRIOR. Who are you?

HARPER. What are you doing in my hallucination?

PRIOR. I'm not in your hallucination. You're in my dream.

HARPER. You're wearing make-up.

PRIOR. So are you.

HARPER. But you're a man.

PRIOR (*feigning horror and dismay, he mimes slashing his throat with his lipstick and dies, fabulously tragic. Then*). The hands and feet give it away.

HARPER. There must be some mistake here. I don't recognise you. You're not . . . Are you my . . . some sort of imaginary friend?

PRIOR. No. Aren't you too old to have imaginary friends?

HARPER. I have emotional problems. I took too many pills. Why are you wearing make-up?

PRIOR. I was in the process of applying the face, trying to make myself feel better – I swiped the new Fall colours at the Clinique counter at Macy's . . . (*Showing her.*)

HARPER. You stole these?

PRIOR. I was out of cash; it was an emotional emergency!

HARPER. Joe will be so angry. I promised him. No more pills.

PRIOR. These pills you keep alluding to?

HARPER. Valium. I take valium. Lots of valium.

PRIOR. And you're dancing as fast as you can.

HARPER. I'm not *addicted*. I don't believe in addiction, and I never . . . well, I *never* drink. And I *never* take drugs.

PRIOR. Well, smell *you*, Nancy Drew.

HARPER. Except valium.

PRIOR. Except valium; in wee fistfuls.

HARPER. It's terrible. Mormons are not supposed to be addicted to anything. I'm a Mormon.

PRIOR. I'm a homosexual.

HARPER. Oh! In my church we don't believe in homosexuals.

PRIOR. In my church we don't believe in Mormons.

HARPER. What church do . . . oh! (*She laughs.*) I get it.
I don't understand this. If I didn't ever see you before and I
don't think I did, then I don't think you should be here, in this
hallucination, because in my experience the mind, which is
where hallucinations come from, shouldn't be able to make up
anything that wasn't there to start with, that didn't enter it
from experience, from the real world. Imagination can't create
anything new, can it? It only recycles bits and pieces from the
world and reassembles them into visions . . . Am I making sense
right now?

PRIOR. Given the circumstances, yes.

HARPER. So when we think we've escaped the unbearable
ordinariness and, well, untruthfulness of our lives, it's really
only the same old ordinariness and falseness rearranged into
the appearance of novelty and truth. Nothing unknown is
knowable. Don't you think it's depressing?

PRIOR. The limitations of the imagination?

HARPER. Yes.

PRIOR. It's something you learn after your second theme party:
It's All Been Done Before.

HARPER. The world. Finite. Terribly, terribly . . . Well . . .
This is the most depressing hallucination I've ever had.

PRIOR. Apologies. I do try to be amusing.

HARPER. Oh, well, don't apologise, you . . . I can't expect
someone who's really sick to entertain me.

PRIOR. How on earth did you know . . .

HARPER. Oh that happens. This is the very threshold of
revelation sometimes. You can see things . . . how sick you are.
Do you see anything about me?

PRIOR. Yes.

HARPER. What?

PRIOR. You are amazingly unhappy.

HARPER. Oh big deal. You meet a valium addict and you figure
out she's unhappy. That doesn't count. Of course I . . .
Something else. Something surprising.

PRIOR. Something surprising.

HARPER. Yes.

PRIOR. Your husband's a homo.

*Pause.*

HARPER. Oh, ridiculous.

*Pause, then very quietly.*

Really?

PRIOR (*shrugs*). Threshold of revelation.

HARPER. Well I don't like your revelations. I don't think you
intuit well at all. Joe's a very normal man, he . . .
Oh God. Oh God. He . . . Do homos take, like, lots of long
walks?

PRIOR. Yes. We do. In stretch pants with lavender coifs, up and
down the avenues of Sodom and Gomorrah, tripping along,
light in our loafers . . .
I just looked at you, and there was . . .

HARPER. A sort of blue streak of recognition.

PRIOR. Yes.

HARPER. Like you knew me incredibly well.

PRIOR. Yes.

HARPER. Yes.
I have to go now, get back, something just . . . fell apart. Oh
God, I feel so sad . . .

PRIOR. I . . . I'm sorry. I usually say, 'Fuck the truth', but mostly,
the truth fucks you.

HARPER. I see something else about you . . .

PRIOR. Oh?

HARPER. Deep inside you, there's a part of you, the most inner
part, entirely free of disease. I can see that.

PRIOR. Is that . . . That isn't true.

HARPER. Threshold of revelation.
Home . . .

HARPER *vanishes.*

PRIOR. People come and go so strangely here . . .
(*To himself in the mirror.*) I don't think there's any uninfected
part of me. My heart is pumping polluted blood. I feel dirty.

*He begins to wipe make-up off with his hands, smearing it around. A
large grey feather falls from up above. PRIOR stops smearing the
make-up and looks at the feather. He goes to it and picks it up.*

A VOICE (*it is an incredibly beautiful voice*). Look up!

PRIOR (*looking up, not seeing anyone*). Hello?

A VOICE. Look up!

PRIOR. Who is that?

A VOICE. Prepare the way!

PRIOR. I don't see any . . .

*There is a dramatic change in lighting, from above.*

A VOICE. Look up, look up,
    prepare the way
    the infinite descent
    A breath in air
    floating down
    Glory to . . . (*Silence.*)

PRIOR. Hello? Is that it? Helloooo!
    What the fuck . . .? (*He holds himself.*)
    Poor me. Poor poor me. Why me? Why poor poor me?
    Oh I don't feel good right now. I really don't.


**Scene Eight**

*Split scene:* HARPER *and* JOE *at home;* PRIOR *and* LOUIS *in bed.*

HARPER. Where were you?

JOE. Out.

HARPER. Where?

JOE. Just out. Thinking.

HARPER. It's late.

JOE. I had a lot to think about.

HARPER. I burned dinner.

JOE. Sorry.

HARPER. Not my dinner. My dinner was fine. Your dinner. I put it back in the oven and turned everything up as high as it could go and I watched till it burned black. It's still hot. Very hot. Want it?

JOE. You didn't have to do that.

HARPER. I know. It just seemed like the kind of thing a mentally-deranged sex-starved pill-popping housewife would do.

JOE. Uh huh.

HARPER. So I did it. Who knows anymore what I have to do?

JOE. How many pills?

HARPER. A bunch. Don't change the subject.

JOE. I won't talk to you when you . . .

HARPER. No. No. Don't do that! I'm . . . I'm fine, pills are not the problem, not our problem, I WANT TO KNOW WHERE YOU'VE BEEN! I WANT TO KNOW WHAT'S GOING ON!

JOE. Going on with what? The job?

HARPER. Not the job.

JOE. I said I need more time.

HARPER. Not the job!

JOE. Mr Cohn, I talked to him on the phone, he said I had to hurry . . .

HARPER. Not the . . .

JOE. But I can't get you to talk sensibly about anything so . . .

HARPER. SHUT UP!

JOE. Then what?

HARPER. Stick to the subject.

JOE. I don't know what that is. You have something you want to ask me? Ask me. Go.

HARPER. I . . . can't. I'm scared of you.

JOE. I'm tired, I'm going to bed.

HARPER. Tell me without making me ask. Please.

JOE. This is crazy, I'm not . . .

HARPER. When you come through the door at night your face is
never exactly the way I remembered it. I get surprised by
something . . . mean and hard about the way you look. Even
the weight of you in the bed at night, the way you breath in
your sleep seems unfamiliar.
   You terrify me.

JOE. I know who you are.

HARPER. Yes. I'm the enemy. That's easy. That doesn't change.
   You think you're the only one who hates sex; I do; I hate it
with you; I do; I'm glad we don't do it anymore. I dream that
you batter away at me till all my joints come apart, like wax,
and I fall into pieces. It's like a punishment. It was wrong of
me to marry you. I knew you . . . (*She stops herself.*) It's a sin,
and it's killing us both.

JOE. I can always tell when you've taken pills because it makes
you red-faced and sweaty and frankly that's very often why I
don't want to . . .

HARPER. Because . . .

JOE. Well, you aren't pretty. Not like this.

HARPER. I have something to ask you.

JOE. Then ASK! ASK! What in hell are you . . .

HARPER. Are you a homo?

*Pause.*

Are you? If you try to walk out right now I'll put your dinner
back in the oven and turn it up so high the whole building will
fill with smoke and everyone in it will asphyxiate. So help me
God I will.
   Now answer the question.

JOE. What if I . . .

*Small pause.*

HARPER. Then tell me, please. And we'll see.

JOE. No. I'm not.
   I don't see what difference it makes.

LOUIS. Jews don't have any clear textual guide to the afterlife; even that it exists. I don't think much about it. I see it as a perpetual rainy Thursday afternoon in March. Dead leaves.

PRIOR. Eeeugh. Very Greco-Roman.

LOUIS. Well for us it's not the verdict that counts, it's the act of judgement. That's why I could never be a lawyer. In court all that matters is the verdict.

PRIOR. You could never be a lawyer because you are oversexed. Too distracted.

LOUIS. Not distracted; *ab*stracted. I'm trying to make a point:

PRIOR. Namely:

LOUIS. It's the judge in his or her chambers, weighing, books open, pondering the evidence, ranging freely over categories: good, evil, innocent, guilty; the judge in the chamber of circumspection, not the judge on the bench with the gavel. The shaping of the law, not its execution.

PRIOR. The point, dear, the point . . .

LOUIS. That it should be the questions and shape of a life, its total complexity gathered, arranged and considered, which matters in the end, not some stamp of salvation or damnation which disperses all the complexity in some unsatisfying little decision – the balancing of the scales . . .

PRIOR. I like this; very Zen; it's . . . reassuringly incomprehensible and useless. We who are about to die thank you.

LOUIS. You are not about to die.

PRIOR. It's not going well, really . . . two new lesions. My leg hurts. There's protein in my urine, the doctor says, but who knows what the fuck that portends. Anyway it shouldn't be there, the protein. My butt is chapped from diarrhoea and yesterday I shat blood.

LOUIS. I really hate this. You don't tell me . . .

PRIOR. You get too upset, I wind up comforting you. It's easier . . .

LOUIS. Oh thanks.

PRIOR. If it's bad I'll tell you.

LOUIS. Shitting blood sounds bad to me.

PRIOR. And I'm telling you.

LOUIS. And I'm handling it.

PRIOR. Tell me some more about justice.

LOUIS. I *am* handling it.

PRIOR. Well Louis you win Trooper of the Month.

LOUIS *starts to cry.*

PRIOR. I take it back. You aren't Trooper of the Month.
This isn't working . . .
Tell me some more about justice.

LOUIS. You are not about to die.

PRIOR. Justice . . .

LOUIS. . . . is an immensity, a confusing vastness. Justice is God.
Prior?

PRIOR. Hmmm?

LOUIS. You love me.

PRIOR. Yes.

LOUIS. What if I walked out on this?
Would you hate me forever?

PRIOR *kisses* LOUIS *on the forehead.*

PRIOR. Yes.

JOE. I think we ought to pray. Ask God for help. Ask him
together . . .

HARPER. God won't talk to me. I have to make up people to talk
to me.

JOE. You have to keep asking.

HARPER. I forgot the question.
Oh yeah. God, is my husband a . . .

JOE. Stop it. Stop it. I'm warning you.
Does it make any difference? That I might be one thing deep
within, no matter how wrong or ugly that thing is, so long as I
have fought, with everything I have, to kill it. What do you
want from me? What do you want from me, Harper? More
than that? For God's sake, there's nothing left, I'm a shell.
There's nothing left to kill.

As long as my behaviour is what I know it has to be. Decent.
Correct. That alone in the eyes of God.

HARPER. No, no, not that, that's Utah talk, Mormon talk, I hate
it. Joe, tell me, say it . . .

JOE. All I will say is that I am a very good man who has worked
very hard to become good and you want to destroy that. You
want to destroy me, but I am not going to let you do that.

*Pause.*

HARPER. I'm going to have a baby.

JOE. Liar.

HARPER. You liar.
A baby born addicted to pills. A baby who does not dream
but who hallucinates, who stares up at us with big mirror eyes
and who does not know who we are.

*Pause.*

JOE. Are you really . . .

HARPER. No. Yes. No. Yes. Get away from me.
Now we both have a secret.


PRIOR. One of my ancestors was a ship's captain who made
money bringing whale oil to Europe and returning with
immigrants – Irish mostly, packed in tight, so many dollars per
head. The last ship he captained foundered off the coast of
Nova Scotia in a winter tempest and sank to the bottom. He
went down with the ship – La Grande Geste – but his crew took
seventy women and kids in the ship's only longboat, this big,
open rowboat, and when the weather got too rough, and they
thought the boat was overcrowded, the crew started lifting
people up and hurling them into the sea. Until they got the
ballast right. They walked up and down the longboat, eyes to
the waterline, and when the boat rode low in the water they'd
grab the nearest passenger and throw them into the sea. The
boat was leaky, see; seventy people; they arrived in Halifax with
nine people on board.

LOUIS. Jesus.

PRIOR. I think about that story a lot now. People in a boat,
waiting, terrified, while implacable, unsmiling men, irresistibly
strong, seize . . . maybe the person next to you, maybe you, and

with no warning at all, with time only for a quick intake of air you are pitched into freezing, turbulent water and salt and darkness to drown.

I like your cosmology, baby. While time is running out I find myself drawn to anything that's suspended, that lacks an ending – but it seems to me that it lets you off scot free.

LOUIS. What do you mean?

PRIOR. No judgement, no guilt or responsibility.

LOUIS. For me.

PRIOR. For anyone. It was an editorial 'you'.

LOUIS. Please get better. Please.
Please don't get any sicker.

**Scene Nine**

ROY *and* HENRY, *his doctor, in* HENRY's *office.*

HENRY. Nobody knows what causes it. And nobody knows how to cure it. The best theory is that we blame a retrovirus, the Human Immunodeficiency Virus. Its presence is made known to us by the useless antibodies which appear in reaction to its entrance into the bloodstream through a cut, or an orifice. The antibodies are powerless to protect the body against it. Why, we don't know. The body's immune system ceases to function. Sometimes the body even attacks itself. At any rate it's left open to a whole horror house of infections from microbes which it usually defends against.

Like Kaposi's Sarcomas. These lesions. Or your throat problem. Or the glands.

We think it may also be able to slip past the blood-brain barrier into the brain. Which is of course very bad news. And it's fatal in we don't know what percent of people with suppressed immune responses.

*Pause.*

ROY. This is very interesting, Mr Wizard, but why the fuck are you telling me this?

*Pause.*

HENRY. Well, I have just removed one of three lesions which
biopsy results will probably tell us is a Kaposi's Sarcoma lesion.
And you have a pronounced swelling of glands in your neck,
groin, and armpits – Lymphadenopathy is another sign. And
you have oral candidiasis and maybe a little more fungus under
the fingernails of two digits on your right hand. So that's
why . . .

ROY. This disease . . .

HENRY. Syndrome.

ROY. Whatever. It afflicts mostly homosexuals and drug addicts.

HENRY. Mostly. Haemophiliacs are also at risk.

ROY. Homosexuals and drug addicts. So why are you implying
that I . . .

*Pause.*

What are you implying, Henry?

HENRY. Roy . . .

ROY. I'm not a drug addict.

HENRY. Oh come on Roy.

ROY. What, what, come on Roy what? Do you think I'm a junkie,
Henry, do you see tracks?

HENRY. This is absurd.

ROY. Say it.

HENRY. Say what?

ROY. Say, 'Roy Cohn, you are a . . .'

HENRY. Roy.

ROY. 'You are a . . .' Go on. Not 'Roy Cohn you are a drug
fiend.' 'Roy Marcus Cohn, you are a . . .'
Go on, Henry, it starts with an 'H'.

HENRY. Oh I'm not going to . . .

ROY. *With an 'H'*, Henry, and it isn't 'Haemophiliac.' Come
on . . .

HENRY. What are you doing, Roy?

ROY. No, say it. I mean it. Say: 'Roy Cohn, you are a
homosexual.'

*Pause.*

And I will proceed, systematically, to destroy your reputation and your practice and your career in New York State, Henry. Which you know I can do.

*Pause.*

HENRY. Roy, you have been seeing me since 1958. Apart from the face-lifts I have treated you for everything from syphilis . . .

ROY. From a whore in Dallas.

HENRY. From syphilis to venereal warts. In your rectum. Which you may have gotten from a whore in Dallas, but it wasn't a female whore.

*Pause.*

ROY. So say it.

HENRY. Roy Cohn, you are . . .
    You have had sex with men, many many times, Roy, and one of them, or any number of them, has made you very sick. You have AIDS.

ROY. AIDS.
    Your problem, Henry, is that you are hung up on words, on labels, that you believe they mean what they seem to mean. AIDS. Homosexual. Gay. Lesbian. You think these are names that tell you who someone sleeps with, but they don't tell you that.

HENRY. No?

ROY. No. Like all labels they tell you one thing and one thing only: where does an individual so identified fit in the food chain, in the pecking order? Not ideology, or sexual taste, but something much simpler: clout. Not who I fuck or who fucks me, but who will pick up the phone when I call, who owes me favours. This is what a label refers to. Now to someone who does not understand this, homosexual is what I am because I have sex with men. But really this is wrong. Homosexuals are not men who sleep with other men. Homosexuals are men who in fifteen years of trying cannot get a pissante anti-discrimination bill through City Council. Homosexuals are men who know nobody and who nobody knows. Who have zero clout. Does this sound like me, Henry?

HENRY. No.

ROY. No. I have clout. A lot. I can pick up this phone, punch
fifteen numbers, and you know who will be on the other end in
under five minutes, Henry?

HENRY. The President.

ROY. Even better, Henry. His wife.

HENRY. I'm impressed.

ROY. I don't want you to be impressed. I want you to
understand. This is not sophistry. And this is not hypocrisy.
This is reality. I have sex with men. But unlike nearly every
other man of whom this is true, I bring the guy I'm screwing to
the White House and President Reagan smiles at us and shakes
his hand. Because *what* I am is defined entirely by *who* I am.
Roy Cohn is not a homosexual. Roy Cohn is a heterosexual
man, Henry, who fucks around with guys.

HENRY. OK, Roy.

ROY. And what is my diagnosis, Henry?

HENRY. You have AIDS, Roy.

ROY. No, Henry, no. AIDS is what homosexuals have. I have
liver cancer.

*Pause.*

HENRY. Well, whatever the fuck you have, Roy, it's very serious,
and I haven't got a damn thing for you. The NIH Hospital in
Bethesda has some experimental treatments with two-year
waiting lists that not even I can get you onto. So get on the
phone, Roy, and dial the fifteen numbers, and tell the First
Lady you need in on an experimental treatment for liver
cancer, because you can call it any damn thing you want, Roy,
but what it boils down to is very bad news.

## ACT TWO: IN VITRO   Early Winter 1985

### Scene One

PRIOR *alone on the floor of his bedroom; he is much worse.*

PRIOR. Louis, Louis, please wake up, oh God.

   LOUIS *runs in.*

PRIOR. I think something horrible is wrong with me I can't
   breathe . . .

LOUIS (*starting to exit*). I'm calling the ambulance.

PRIOR. No, wait, I . . .

LOUIS. *Wait?* Are you fucking crazy? Oh God you're on fire,
   your head is on fire.

PRIOR. It hurts, it hurts . . .

LOUIS. I'm calling the ambulance.

PRIOR. I don't want to go to the hospital, I don't want to go to
   the hospital please let me lie here, just . . .

LOUIS. No, no, God, Prior, stand up . . .

PRIOR. DON'T TOUCH MY LEG!

LOUIS. We have to . . . oh God this is so crazy.

PRIOR. I'll be OK if I just lie here Lou, really, if I can only sleep
   a little . . .

   LOUIS *exits.*

PRIOR. Louis?
   NO! NO! Don't call, you'll send me there and I won't come
   back, please, please Louis I'm begging, baby, please . . .
   (*Screams.*) LOUIS!!

LOUIS (*from off, hysterical*). WILL YOU SHUT THE FUCK UP!

PRIOR (*trying to stand*). Aaaah. I have . . . to go to the bathroom.
   Wait. Wait, just . . . oh.
   Oh God. (*He shits himself.*)

LOUIS (*entering*). Prior? They'll be here in . . .
  Oh my God.

PRIOR. I'm sorry, I'm sorry.

LOUIS. What did . . .? What?

PRIOR. I had an accident.

  LOUIS *goes to him.*

LOUIS. This is blood.

PRIOR. Maybe you shouldn't touch it . . . me . . . I . . . (*He faints.*)

LOUIS (*quietly*). Oh help. Oh help. Oh God oh God oh God help
  me I can't I can't I can't.

## Scene Two

**HARPER** *is sitting at home at night, all alone, with no lights on. We
can barely see her.* JOE *enters, but he doesn't turn on the lights.*

JOE. Why are you sitting in the dark? Turn on the light.

HARPER. *No.* I heard the sounds in the bedroom again. I know
  someone was in there.

JOE. No one was.

HARPER. Maybe actually in the bed, under the covers with a
  knife.
    Oh, boy. Joe. I, um, I'm thinking of going away. By which I
  mean: I think I'm going off again. You . . . you know what I
  mean?

JOE. Please don't. Stay. We can fix it. I pray for that. This is my
  fault, but I can correct it. You have to try too . . .

  *He turns on the light. She turns it off again.*

HARPER. When you pray, what do you pray for?

JOE. I pray for God to crush me, break me up into little pieces
  and start all over again.

HARPER. Oh. Please. Don't pray for that.

JOE. I had a book of Bible stories when I was a kid. There was a
  picture I'd look at twenty times every day: Jacob wrestles with

the angel. I don't really remember the story, or why the
wrestling – just the picture. Jacob is young and very strong.
The angel is . . . a beautiful man, with golden hair and wings,
of course. I still dream about it. Many nights. I'm . . . It's me.
In that struggle. Fierce, and unfair. The angel is not human,
and it holds nothing back, so how could anyone human win,
what kind of a fight is that? It's not just. Losing means your
soul thrown down in the dust, your heart torn out from God's.
But you can't not lose.

HARPER. In the whole entire world, you are the only person,
the only person I love or have ever loved. And I love you
terribly. Terribly. That's what's so awfully, irreducibly real. I
can make up anything but I can't dream that away.

JOE. Are you . . . are you really going to have a baby?

HARPER. It's my time, and there's no blood. I don't really know.
I suppose it wouldn't be a great thing. Maybe I'm just not
bleeding because I take too many pills. Maybe I'll give birth to
a pill. That would give a new meaning to pill-popping, huh?
    I think you should go to Washington. Alone. Change, like
you said.

JOE. I'm not going to leave you, Harper.

HARPER. Well maybe not. But I'm going to leave you.

## Scene Three

LOUIS *and a nurse*, EMILY, *are sitting in* PRIOR's *room in the
hospital, same night as Scene One but much later.*

EMILY. He'll be alright now.

LOUIS. No he won't.

EMILY. No. I guess not. I gave him something that makes him
sleep.

LOUIS. Deep asleep?

EMILY. Orbiting the moons of Jupiter.

LOUIS. A good place to be.

EMILY. Anyplace better than here. You his . . . uh?

LOUIS. Yes I'm his uh.

EMILY. This must be hell for you.

LOUIS. It is. Hell. The After Life. Which is not at all like a rainy
afternoon in March, by the way, Prior. A lot more vivid than
I'd expected. Dead leaves, but the crunchy kind. Sharp, dry air.
The kind of long, luxurious dying feeling that breaks your
heart.

EMILY. Yeah, well we all get to break our hearts on this one.
He seems like a nice guy. Cute.

LOUIS. Not like this.
Yes, he is. Was. Whatever.

EMILY. Weird name. Prior Walter. Like, 'The Walter before this
one.'

LOUIS. Lots of Walters before this one. Prior is an old old family
name in an old old family. The Walters go back to the
Mayflower and beyond. Back to the Norman Conquests. He
says there's a Prior Walter stitched into the Bayeux Tapestry.

EMILY. Is that impressive?

LOUIS. Well, it's old. Very old. Which in some circles equals
impressive.

EMILY. Not in my circle. What's the name of the tapestry?

LOUIS. The Bayeux Tapestry. Embroidered by La Reine
Mathilde.

EMILY. I'll tell my mother. She embroiders. Drives me nuts.

LOUIS. Manual therapy for anxious hands.

EMILY. Maybe you should try it.

LOUIS. Mathilde stitched while William the Conqueror was off to
war. She was capable of . . . more than loyalty. Devotion.
She waited for him, she stitched for years. And if he had
come back broken and defeated from war, she would have
loved him even more. And if he had returned mutilated, ugly,
full of infection and horror, she would still have loved him; fed
by pity, by a sharing of pain, she would love him even more,
and even more, and she would never, never have prayed to
God, please let him die if he can't return to me whole and
healthy and able to live a normal life . . . If he had died, she
would have buried her heart with him.
So what the fuck is the matter with me?

*Little pause.*

Will he sleep through the night?

EMILY. At least.

LOUIS. I'm going.

EMILY. It's two a.m. Where do you have to go at . . .

LOUIS. I know what time it is. A walk. Night air, good for
the . . . The park.

EMILY. Be careful.

LOUIS. Yeah. Danger.
    Tell him, if he wakes up and you're still on, tell him goodbye,
tell him I had to go.

## Scene Four

**Split scene:** *JOE and ROY in a fancy (straight) bar; LOUIS and a
MAN in the Rambles in Central Park. JOE and ROY are sitting at a
table; the place is brightly lit. JOE has a plate of food in front of him but
he isn't eating. ROY occasionally reaches over the table and forks small
bites off of JOE's plate. ROY is drinking heavily, JOE not at all.
LOUIS and the MAN are eyeing each other, each alternating interest
and indifference.*

JOE. The pills were something she started when she miscarried
or . . . no, she took some before that. She had a really bad time
at home, when she was a kid, her home was really bad. I think
a lot of drinking and physical stuff. She doesn't talk about that,
instead she talks about . . . the sky falling down, people with
knives hiding under sofas. Monsters. Mormons. Everyone
thinks Mormons don't come from homes like that, we aren't
supposed to behave that way, but we do. It's not lying, or being
two-faced. Everyone tries very hard to live up to God's
strictures, which are very . . . um . . .

ROY. Strict.

JOE. I shouldn't be bothering you with this.

ROY. No, please. Heart to heart. Want another . . . what is that,
seltzer?

JOE. The failure to measure up hits people very hard. From such a strong desire to be good they feel very far from goodness when they fail.

What scares me is that maybe what I really love in her is the part of her that's farthest from the light, from God's love, maybe I was drawn to that in the first place. And I'm keeping it alive because I need it.

ROY. Why would you need it?

JOE. There are things . . . I don't know how well we know ourselves. I mean, what if? I know I married her because she . . . because I loved it that she was always wrong, always doing something wrong, like one step out of step. In Salt Lake City that stands out. I never stood out, on the outside, but inside, it was hard for me. To pass.

ROY. Pass?

JOE. Yeah.

ROY. Pass as what?

JOE. Oh. Well . . . As someone cheerful and strong. Those who love God with an open heart unclouded by secrets and struggles are cheerful; God's easy simple love for them shows in how strong and happy they are. The saints.

ROY. But you had secrets? Secret struggles . . .

JOE. I wanted to be one of the elect, one of the Blessed. You feel you ought to be, that the blemishes are yours by choice, which of course they aren't. Harper's sorrow, that really deep sorrow, she didn't choose that. But it's there.

ROY. You didn't put it there.

JOE. No.

ROY. You sound like you think you did.

JOE. I am responsible for her.

ROY. Because she's your wife.

JOE. That. And I do love her.

ROY. Whatever. She's your wife. And so there are obligations. To her. But also to yourself.

JOE. She'd fall apart in Washington.

ROY. Then let her stay here.

JOE. She'll fall apart if I leave her.

ROY. Then bring her to Washington.

JOE. I just can't, Roy. She needs me.

ROY. Listen, Joe. I'm the best divorce lawyer in the business.

*Little pause.*

JOE. Can't Washington wait?

ROY. You do what you need to do, Joe. What *you* need. *You.* Let her life go where it wants to go. You'll both be better for that. *Somebody* should get what they want.

MAN. What do you want?

LOUIS. I want you to fuck me, hurt me, make me bleed.

MAN. I want to.

LOUIS. Yeah?

MAN. I want to hurt you.

LOUIS. Fuck me.

MAN. Yeah?

LOUIS. Hard.

MAN. Yeah? You been a bad boy?

*Pause,* LOUIS *laughs, softly.*

LOUIS. Very bad. Very bad.

MAN. You need to be punished, boy?

LOUIS. Yes. I do.

MAN. Yes what?

*Little pause.*

LOUIS. Um, I . . .

MAN. Yes *what,* boy?

LOUIS. Oh. Yes sir.

MAN. I want you to take me to your place, boy.

LOUIS. No, I can't do that.

MAN. No *what?*

LOUIS. No sir, I can't, I . . .
 I don't live alone, sir.

MAN. Your lover know you're out with a man tonight, boy?

LOUIS. No sir, he . . .
 My lover doesn't know.

MAN. Your lover know you . . .

LOUIS. Let's change the subject, OK? Can we go to your place?

MAN. I live with my parents.

LOUIS. Oh.

ROY. Everyone who makes it in this world makes it because
 somebody older and more powerful takes an interest. The most
 precious asset in life, I think, is the ability to be a good son.
 You have that, Joe. Somebody who can be a good son to a
 father who pushes them farther than they would otherwise go.
 I've had many fathers, I owe my life to them, powerful,
 powerful men. Joe McCarthy most of all. He valued me
 because I am a good lawyer, but he loved me because I was and
 am a good son. He was a very difficult man, very guarded and
 cagey; I brought out something tender in him. He would have
 died for me. And me for him. Does this embarrass you?

JOE. I had a hard time with my father.

ROY. Well sometimes that's the way. Then you have to find other
 fathers, substitutes, I don't know. The father-son relationship is
 central to life. Women are for birth, beginning, but the father
 is continuance. The son offers the father his life as a vessel for
 carrying forth his father's dream. Your father's living?

JOE. Um, dead.

ROY. He was . . . what? A difficult man?

JOE. He was in the military. He could be very unfair. And cold.

ROY. But he loved you.

JOE. I don't know.

ROY. No, no, Joe, he did. I know this. Sometimes a father's love
 has to be very, very hard, unfair even, cold to make his son
 grow strong in a world like this. This isn't a good world.

MAN. Here, then.

LOUIS. I . . . Do you have a rubber?

MAN. I don't use rubbers.

LOUIS. You should. (*He takes one from his coat pocket.*) Here.

MAN. I don't use them.

LOUIS. Forget it, then. (*He starts to leave.*)

MAN. No, wait.
Put it on me. Boy.

LOUIS. Forget it, I have to get back. Home. I must be going
crazy.

MAN. Oh come on please he won't find out.

LOUIS. It's cold. Too cold.

MAN. It's never too cold, let me warm you up. Please?

*They begin to fuck.*

MAN. Relax.

LOUIS (*a small laugh*). Not a chance.

MAN. It . . .

LOUIS. What?

MAN. I think it broke. The rubber. You want me to pull out?

*Pause.*

LOUIS.   Keep . . . keep going.
Inject me.
I don't care. I don't care.

*Pause. The man pulls out.*

MAN. I . . . um, look, I'm sorry, but I think I want to go.

LOUIS. Yeah.
Give my best to Mom and Dad.

*The man slaps him.*

LOUIS. Ow!

*They stare at each other.*

LOUIS. It was a joke.

*The man leaves.*

ROY. How long have we known each other?

JOE. Since 1980.

ROY. Right. A long time. I feel close to you, Joe. Do I advise you well?

JOE. You've been an incredible friend, Roy, I . . .

ROY. I want to be family. Familia, as my Italian friends call it. La Familia. A lovely word. It's important for me to help you, like I was helped.

JOE. I owe practically everything to you, Roy.

ROY. I'm dying, Joe. Cancer.

JOE. Oh my God.

ROY. Please. Let me finish.
   Few people know this and I'm telling you this only because . . . I'm not afraid of death. What can death bring that I haven't faced? I've lived; life is the worst. Listen to me, I'm a philosopher.
   Joe. You must do this. You must must must. Love; that's a trap. Responsibility; that's a trap too. Like a father to a son I tell you this: Life is full of horror; nobody escapes, nobody; save yourself. Whatever pulls on you, whatever needs from you, threatens you. Don't be afraid; people are so afraid; don't be afraid to live in the raw wind, naked, alone . . . Learn at least this: What you are capable of. Let nothing stand in your way.


**Scene Five**

PRIOR *and* BELIZE *in* PRIOR's *hospital room. Several days after admittance;* PRIOR *is very sick but improving.* BELIZE *has just arrived.*

PRIOR. Miss Thing.

BELIZE. Ma chérie bichette.

PRIOR. Stella.

BELIZE. Stella for star. Let me see. (*Scrutinising* PRIOR.)
   You look like shit, why yes indeed you do, comme la merde!

PRIOR. Merci.

BELIZE (*taking little plastic bottles from his bag, handing them to* PRIOR.) Not to despair, Belle Reeve. Lookie! Magic goop!

PRIOR (*opening a bottle, sniffing*). Pooh! What kinda crap is that?

BELIZE. Beats me. Let's rub it on your poor blistered body and see what it does.

PRIOR. This is not Western medicine, these bottles . . .

BELIZE. Voodoo cream. From the botanica round the block.

PRIOR. And you a registered nurse.

BELIZE (*sniffing it*). Beeswax and cheap perfume. Cut with Jergen's Lotion. Full of good vibes and love from some little black Cubana witch in Miami.

PRIOR. Get that trash away from me, I am immune-suppressed.

BELIZE. I *am* a health professional. I *know* what I'm doing.

PRIOR. It stinks. Any word from Louis?

*Pause.* BELIZE *starts giving* PRIOR *a gentle massage.*

PRIOR. Gone.

BELIZE. He'll be back. I know the type. Likes to keep a girl on edge.

PRIOR. It's been . . .

*Pause.*

BELIZE (*trying to jog his memory*). How long?

PRIOR. I don't remember.

BELIZE. How long have you been here?

PRIOR (*getting suddenly upset*). I don't remember, I don't give a fuck. I want Louis. I want my fucking boyfriend, where the fuck is he? I'm dying, I'm dying, where's Louis?

BELIZE. Ssssh, sssh . . .

PRIOR. This is a very strange drug, this drug. Emotional lability, for starters.

BELIZE. Save a tab or two for me.

PRIOR. Oh no, not this drug, ce n'est pas pour le joyeux noel et la bonne année, this drug she is serious poisonous chemistry,

ma pauvre bichette.
    And not just disorienting. I hear things. Voices.

BELIZE. Voices.

PRIOR. A voice.

BELIZE. Saying what?

*Pause.*

PRIOR. I'm not supposed to tell.

BELIZE. You better tell the doctor. Or I will.

PRIOR. No no don't. Please. I want the voice; it's wonderful. It's all that's keeping me alive. I don't want to talk to some intern about it.
    You know what happens? When I hear it, I get hard.

BELIZE. Oh my.

PRIOR. Comme ça. (*He uses his arm to demonstrate.*) And you know I am slow to rise.

BELIZE. My jaw aches at the memory.

PRIOR. And would you deny me this little solace – betray my concupiscence to Florence Nightingale's storm troopers?

BELIZE. Perish the thought, ma bébé.

PRIOR. They'd change the drug just to spoil the fun.

BELIZE. You and your boner can depend on me.

PRIOR. Je t'adore, ma belle Nègre.

BELIZE. All this girl-talk shit is politically incorrect, you know. We should have dropped it back when we gave up drag.

PRIOR. I'm sick, I get to be politically incorrect if it makes me feel better. You sound like Lou.

*Little pause.*

Well, at least I have the satisfaction of knowing he's in anguish somewhere. I loved his anguish. Watching him stick his head up his asshole and eat his guts out over some relatively minor moral conundrum – it was the best show in town. But mother warned me: if they get overwhelmed by the little things . . .

BELIZE. They'll be belly-up bustville when something big comes along.

PRIOR. Mother warned me.

BELIZE. And they do come along.

PRIOR. But I didn't listen.

BELIZE. No. (*As Hepburn.*) Men are beasts.

PRIOR (*also Hepburn*). The absolute lowest.

BELIZE. I have to go. If I want to spend my whole lonely life looking after white people I can get underpaid to do it.

PRIOR. You're just a Christian martyr.

BELIZE. Whatever happens, baby, I will be here for you.

PRIOR. Je t'aime.

BELIZE. Je t'aime. Don't go crazy on me, girlfriend, I already got enough crazy queens for one lifetime. For two. I can't be bothering with dementia.

PRIOR. I promise.

BELIZE (*touching him; softly*). Ouch.

PRIOR. Ouch. Indeed.

BELIZE. Why'd they have to pick on you?
    And eat more, girlfriend, you really do look like shit.
    (*He leaves.*)

PRIOR (*after waiting a beat.*) He's gone.
    Are you still . . .

VOICE. I can't stay. I will return.

PRIOR. Are you one of those 'Follow me to the other side' voices?

VOICE. No I am no nightbird. I am a messenger . . .

PRIOR. You have a beautiful voice, it sounds . . . like a viola, like a perfectly tuned, tight string, balanced, the truth . . . Stay with me.

VOICE. Not now. Soon I will return, I will reveal myself to you; I am glorious, glorious; my heart, my countenance and my message. You must prepare.

PRIOR. For what? I don't want to . . .

VOICE. No death, no:
    A marvellous work and a wonder we undertake, an edifice

awry we sink plumb and straighten, a great Lie we abolish, a
great error correct, with the rule, sword and broom of Truth!

PRIOR. What are you talking about, I . . .

VOICE. I am on my way; when I am manifest, our Work begins:
Prepare for the parting of the air,
The breath, the ascent,
Glory to . . .


**Scene Six**

MARTIN, ROY *and* JOE *in a fancy Manhattan restaurant.*

MARTIN. It's a revolution in Washington, Joe. We have a new
agenda and finally a real leader. They got back the Senate but
we have the courts. By the nineties the Supreme Court will be
block solid Republican appointees, and the Federal bench –
Republican judges like land mines, everywhere, everywhere
they turn. Affirmative action? Take it to court. Boom! Land
mine. And we'll get our way on just about everything: abortion,
defence, Central America, protecting the family, a live
investment climate. We have the White House locked till the
year 2000. And beyond. A permanent fix on the Oval Office?
It's possible. By '92 we'll get the Senate back, and in ten years
the South is going to give us the House. It's really the end of
Liberalism. The end of New Deal Socialism. The end of ipso
facto secular humanism. The dawning of a genuinely American
political personality. Modelled on Ronald Wilson Reagan.

JOE. It sounds great, Mr Heller.

MARTIN. Martin. And Justice is the hub. Especially since Ed
Meese took over. He doesn't specialise in Fine Points in the
Law. He's a flatfoot, a cop. He reminds me of Teddy Roosevelt.

JOE. I can't wait to meet him.

MARTIN. Too bad, Joe, he's been dead for sixty years!

*There is a little awkwardness.* JOE *doesn't respond.*

MARTIN. Teddy Roosevelt. You said you wanted to . . . Little
joke.

ROY (*smiling, but nasty*). Aw shut the fuck up Martin.

(*To Joe.*) Mr Heller here is one of the mighty, Joseph, in D.C. he sitteth on the right hand of the man who sitteth on the right hand of The Man. And yet I can say 'shut the fuck up' and he will take offence. Loyalty. He . . . Martin?

MARTIN. Yes, Roy?

ROY. Rub my back.

MARTIN. Roy . . .

ROY. No, no, really, a sore spot, I get them all the time now, these . . . Rub it for me darling, would you do that for me?

MARTIN *rubs* ROY's *back. They both look at* JOE.

ROY (*to* JOE). Comrades. How the hell else do you think a handful of Bolsheviks turned St Petersburg into Leningrad in one afternoon? Fucking certain *God* had nothing to do with it. *Comrades*, right Martin?

MARTIN. This man, Joe, is a Saint of the Right.

JOE. I know, Mr Heller, I . . .

ROY. And you see what mean, Martin? He's special, right?

MARTIN. Don't embarrass him, Roy.

ROY. Gravity, decency, smarts! I'm telling you, his strength is as the strength of ten because his heart if pure! *And* he's a Royboy, one hundred percent.

MARTIN. We're on the move, Joe. On the move.

JOE. Mr Heller, I.

MARTIN (*ending back rub*). We can't wait any longer for an answer.

*Little pause.*

JOE. Oh. Um, I . . .

ROY. Joe's a married man, Martin.

MARTIN. Aha.

ROY. With a wife. She doesn't care to go to D.C., and so Joe cannot go. And keeps us dangling. We've seen that kind of thing before, haven't we? These men and their wives.

MARTIN. Oh yes. Beware.

JOE. I really can't discuss this under . . .

MARTIN. Then *don't* discuss. Say yes, Joe.

ROY. Now.

MARTIN. Say yes I will.

ROY. Now.
    Now. I'll hold my breath till you do, I'm turning blue
    waiting . . . *Now*, goddamit!

MARTIN. Roy, calm down, it's not . . .

ROY. Aw, fuck it.

    ROY *takes a letter from his jacket pocket, hands it to* JOE.

ROY. Read. Came today.

    JOE *reads the first paragraph, then looks up.*

JOE. Roy. This is . . . Roy, this is terrible.

ROY. You're telling me.
    A letter from the American Bar Association, Martin.
    They're gonna try and disbar me.

MARTIN. Oh my.

JOE. Why?

ROY. Why, Martin?

MARTIN. Revenge.

ROY. The whole Establishment. Their little rules. Because I
    know no rules. Because I don't see the Law as a dead and
    arbitrary collection of antiquated dictums, thou shall, thou shalt
    not, because, because I know the Law's a pliable, breathing,
    sweating . . . *organ*, because, because . . .

MARTIN. Because he borrowed half a million from one of his
    clients.

ROY. Yeah, well, there's that.

MARTIN. *And* he forgot to *return* it.

JOE. Roy, that's . . . You borrowed money from a client?

ROY. I'm deeply ashamed.

    *Little pause.*

JOE. Roy, you know how much I admire you. Well I mean I know you have unorthodox ways, but I'm sure you only did what you thought at the time you needed to do. And I have faith that . . .

ROY. Not so damp, please. I'll deny it was a loan. She's got no paperwork. Can't prove a fucking thing.

*Little pause.* MARTIN *studies the menu.*

JOE (*handing back the letter*). Roy I really appreciate your telling me this, and I'll do whatever I can to help.

ROY (*holding up a hand, then, carefully*). I'll tell you what you can do.
 I'm about to be tried, Joe, by a jury that is not a jury of my peers. The disbarment committee: Genteel gentleman Brahmin lawyers, country club men. I offend them, to these men . . . I'm what? Martin, some sort of filthy little Jewish troll?

MARTIN. Oh well, I wouldn't go so far as . . .

ROY. Oh well I would.
 Very fancy lawyers, these disbarment committee lawyers, fancy lawyers with fancy corporate clients and complicated cases. Antitrust suits. Deregulation. Environmental control. Complex cases like these need Justice Department co-operation like flowers need the sun. Wouldn't you say that's an accurate assessment, Martin?

MARTIN. I'm not hearing any of this, Roy. I'm not here.

ROY. No. Of course not.
 Without the light of the sun, Joe, these cases, and the fancy lawyers who represent them, will wither and die.
 A well-placed friend, someone in the Justice Department, say, can turn off the sun. Cast a deep shadow on my behalf. Make them shiver in the cold. If they overstep. They would fear that.

*Pause.*

JOE. Roy. I don't understand.

ROY. You do.

*Pause.*

JOE. You're not asking me to . . .

ROY. Sssshhhh. Careful.

JOE (*a beat, then*). Even if I said yes to the job, it would be illegal to interfere. With the hearings. It's unethical. No. I can't.

ROY. Un-ethical.
Would you excuse us, Martin?

MARTIN. Excuse you?

ROY. Take a walk, Martin. For real.

MARTIN *leaves*.

ROY. Un-ethical. Are you trying to embarrass me in front of my friend?

JOE. Well it is unethical, I can't . . .

ROY. Boy, you are really something, what the fuck do you think this is, Sunday School?

JOE. No, but Roy this is . . .

ROY. This is . . . this is gastric juices churning, this is enzymes and acids, this is intestinal is what this is, bowel movement and blood-red meat – this stinks, this is *politics*, Joe, the game of being alive. And you think you're . . . What? Above that? Above alive is what? Dead! In the clouds! You're on earth, goddamit! Plant a foot, stay a while.
    I'm sick. They smell I'm weak. They want blood this time. I must have eyes in Justice. In Justice you will protect me.

JOE. Why can't Mr Heller . . .

ROY. Grow up, Joe. The administration can't get involved.

JOE. But I'd be part of the administration. The same as him.

ROY. Not the same. Martin's Ed's man. And Ed's Reagan's man.
So Martin's Reagan's man.
And you're mine.

*Little pause. He holds up the letter.*

This will never be? Understand me?

*He tears the leeter up.*

I'm gonna be a lawyer, Joseph, I'm gonna be a lawyer, Joseph, I'm gonna be a goddam motherfucking legally licensed member of the bar lawyer, just like my daddy was, till my last bitter day on earth, Joseph, until the day I die.

MARTIN *returns*.

ROY. Ah, Martin's back.

MARTIN. So are we agreed?

ROY. Joe?

*Little pause.*

JOE. I'll . . . I will think about it. Please. One more day.

MARTIN. It's the fear of what comes after the doing that makes the doing hard to do.

ROY. Amen.

MARTIN. But you can almost always live with the consequences.


## Scene Seven

*On the granite steps outside the Hall of Justice, Brooklyn. It is cold and sunny. A Sabrett wagon is selling hot dogs. LOUIS, in a shabby overcoat, is sitting on the steps contemplatively eating one. JOE enters with three hot dogs and a can of Coke.*

JOE. Can I . . .

LOUIS. Oh sure. Sure. Crazy cold sun.

*JOE sits.*

JOE. Have to make the best of it.
    How's your friend?

LOUIS. My . . .? Oh. He's worse. My friend is worse.

JOE. I'm sorry.

LOUIS. Yeah, well. Thanks for asking. It's nice. You're nice. I can't believe you voted for Reagan.

JOE. I hope he gets better.

LOUIS. Reagan?

JOE. Your friend.

LOUIS. He won't. Neither will Reagan.

JOE. Let's not talk politics, OK?

LOUIS (*pointing to JOE's lunch*). You're eating *three* of those?

JOE. Well . . . I'm . . . hungry.

LOUIS. They're really terrible for you. Full of rat-poo and beetle legs and wood shavings 'n' shit.

JOE. Huh.

LOUIS. And . . . um . . . irridium, I think. Something toxic.

JOE. You're eating one.

LOUIS. Yeah, well, the shape, I can't help myself, plus I'm *trying* to commit suicide, what's your excuse?

JOE. I don't have an excuse. I just have Pepto-Bismol.

*JOE takes a bottle of Pepto Bismol and chugs it. LOUIS shudders audibly.*

Yeah I know but then I wash it down with Coke.

*He does this. LOUIS mimes barfing in his lap.*

Are you *always* like this?

LOUIS. I've been worrying a lot about his kids.

JOE. Whose?

LOUIS. Reagan's. Maureen and Mike and little orphan Patti and Miss Ron Reagan Jr., the you-should-pardon-the-expression heterosexual.

JOE. Ron Reagan Jr. is . . . You shouldn't just make these assumptions about people. How do you know? About him? What he is? You don't know.

LOUIS (*doing Tallulah*). Well darling he never sucked *my* cock but . . .

JOE. Look, if you're going to get vulgar . . .

LOUIS. No no really I mean . . . What's it like to be the child of The Zeitgeist? To have the American Animus as your dad? It's not really a *family*, the Reagans, I read *People*, there aren't any connections there, no love, they don't ever even speak to each other except through their agents. So what's it like to be Reagan's kid? Enquiring minds want to know.

JOE. You can't believe everything you . . .

LOUIS. But . . . I think we all know what that's like. Nowadays. No connections. No responsibilities. All of us . . . falling

through the cracks that separate what we owe to our selves
and . . . and what we owe to love.

*Little pause.*

JOE. You just . . . Whatever you feel like doing, or saying, you
just say it, you don't even give thinking or regrets or morality
or anything a chance, you do it.

LOUIS. Do what?

JOE. It. Whatever. Whatever it is you want to do.

LOUIS. Are you trying to tell me something?

*Little pause, sexual. They stare at each other.* JOE *looks away.*

JOE. No, I'm just observing that you . . .

LOUIS. Impulsive.

JOE. Yes, I mean it must be scary, you . . .

LOUIS (*shrugs*). Land of the free. Home of the brave. Call me
irresponsible.

JOE. It's kind of terrifying.

LOUIS. Yeah, well, freedom is. Heartless, too.

JOE. Oh you're not heartless.

LOUIS. You don't know. Finish your weenie.

LOUIS *pats* JOE *on the knee, starts to leave,*

JOE. Um . . .

LOUIS *turns, looks at him.* JOE *searches for something to say.*

JOE. Yesterday was Sunday but I've been a little unfocused
recently and I thought it was Monday. So I came here like I
was going to work. And the whole place was empty. And at
first I couldn't figure out why, and I had this moment of
incredible . . . fear and also . . . It just flashed through my
mind: The whole Hall of Justice, it's empty, it's deserted, it's
gone out of business. Forever. The people that make it run
have up and abandoned it.

LOUIS (*looking at the building*). Creepy.

JOE. Well yes but. I felt that I was going to scream. Not because
it was creepy, but because the emptiness felt so fast.
And . . . well, good. A . . . happy scream. I just wondered

what a thing it would be . . . if overnight everything you owe anything to, justice, or love, had really gone away. Free.

It would be . . . heartless terror. Yes. Terrible, and . . . Very great. To shed your skin, every old skin, one by one and then walk away, unencumbered, into the morning.

*Little pause. JOE looks at the building.*

I can't go in there today.

LOUIS. Then don't.

JOE. I can't go in, I need . . .
(*He looks for what he needs. He takes a swig of Pepto Bismol.*)
I can't be this anymore. I need . . . a change, I should just . . .

LOUIS (*not a come-on, necessarily; he doesn't want to be alone*). Want some company? For whatever?

*Pause. JOE looks at LOUIS and then looks away, afraid. LOUIS shrugs.*

Sometimes, even if it scares you to death, you have to be willing to break the law. Know what I mean?

*Another little pause.*

JOE. Yes.

LOUIS. I moved out. I moved out on my . . .
I haven't been sleeping well.

JOE. Me neither.

LOUIS *goes up to JOE, licks his napkin and dabs at JOE's mouth.*

LOUIS. Antacid moustache.
(*Points to the building.*) Maybe the court won't convene. Ever again. Maybe we are free. To do whatever.

Children of the new morning, criminal minds. Selfish and greedy and loveless and blind. Reagan's children.

You're scared. So am I. Everybody is in the land of the free. God help us all.


**Scene Eight**

JOE *at a payphone phoning HANNAH at home in Salt Lake City. It is late at night.*

JOE. Mom?

HANNAH. Joe?

JOE. Hi.

HANNAH. You're calling from the street. It's . . . it must be four in the morning. What's happened?

JOE. Nothing, nothing, I . . .

HANNAH. It's Harper. Is Harper . . . Joe? Joe?

JOE. Yeah, hi. No, Harper's fine. Well, no, she's . . . not fine. How are you, Mom?

HANNAH. What's happened?

JOE. I just wanted to talk to you. I, uh, wanted to try something out on you.

HANNAH. Joe, you haven't . . . have you been drinking, Joe?

JOE. Yes ma'am. I'm drunk.

HANNAH. That isn't like you.

JOE. No. I mean, who's to say?

HANNAH. Why are you out on the street at four a.m.? In that crazy city. It's dangerous.

JOE. Actually, Mom, I'm not on the street. I'm near the boathouse in the park.

HANNAH. What park?

JOE. Central Park.

HANNAH. CENTRAL PARK! Oh my Lord. What on earth are you doing in Central Park at this time of night? Are you . . .
    Joe, I think you ought to go home right now. Call me from home.

*Little pause.*

HANNAH. Joe?

JOE. I come here to watch, Mom. Sometimes. Just to watch.

HANNAH. Watch what? What's there to watch at four in the . . .

JOE. Mom, did dad love me?

HANNAH. What?

JOE. Did he?

HANNAH. You ought to go home and call from there.

JOE. Answer.

HANNAH. This is maudlin. I don't like this conversation.

JOE. Yeah, well, it gets worse from here on.

*Pause.*

HANNAH. Joe?

JOE. Mom. Momma. I'm a homosexual, Momma.
Boy, did that come out awkward.

*Pause.*

Hello? Hello?
I'm a homosexual.

*Pause.*

Please, Momma. Say something.

HANNAH. You're old enough to understand that your father
didn't love you without being ridiculous about it.

JOE. What?

HANNAH. You're ridiculous. You're being ridiculous.

JOE. I'm . . .
What?

HANNAH. You really ought to go home now to your wife. I
need to go to bed. This phone call . . . We will just forget this
phone call.

JOE. Mom.

HANNAH. No more talk. Tonight. This . . .
(*Suddenly very angry.*) Drinking is a sin! A sin! I raised you
better than that. (*She hangs up.*)


**Scene Nine**

HARPER *and* JOE *at home.* LOUIS *and* PRIOR *in* PRIOR's
*hospital room.* JOE *and* LOU *have just entered. This should be fast and
obviously furious; overlapping is fine; the proceedings may be a little
confusing but not the final results.*

HARPER. Oh God. Home. The moment of truth has arrived.

JOE. Harper.

LOUIS. I'm going to move out.

PRIOR. The fuck you are.

JOE. Harper. Please listen. I still love you very much. You're still
my best buddy; I'm not going to leave you.

HARPER. No, I don't like the sound of this. I'm leaving.

LOUIS. I'm leaving.
I already have.

JOE. Please listen. Stay. This is really hard. We have to talk.

HARPER. We are talking. Aren't we. Now please shut up. OK?

PRIOR. Bastard. Sneaking off while I'm flat out here, that's low.
If I could get up now I'd beat the holy shit out of you.

JOE. Did you take pills? How many?

HARPER. No pills. Bad for the . . . (*Pats stomach.*)

JOE. You aren't pregnant. I called your gynaecologist.

HARPER. I'm seeing a new gynaecologist.

PRIOR. You have no right to do this.

LOUIS. Oh, that's ridiculous.

PRIOR. No right. It's criminal.

JOE. Forget about that. Just listen. You want the truth. This is
the truth.
    I knew this when I married you. I've known this I guess for
as long as I've known anything, but . . . I don't know, I thought
maybe that with enough effort and will I could change
myself . . . but I can't . . .

PRIOR. Criminal.

LOUIS. There oughta be a law.

PRIOR. There is a law. You'll see.

JOE. I'm losing ground here, I go walking, you want to know
where I walk, I . . . go to the park, or up and down 53rd Street,
or places where . . . And I keep swearing I won't go walking
again, but I just can't.

LOUIS. I need some privacy.

PRIOR. That's new.

LOUIS. Everything's new, Prior.

JOE. I try to tighten my heart into a knot, a snarl, I try to learn to live dead, just numb, but then I see someone I want, and it's like a nail, like a hot spike right through my chest, and I know I'm losing.

PRIOR. Apartment too small for three? Louis and Prior comfy but not Louis and Prior and Prior's disease?

LOUIS. Something like that.
    I won't be judged by you. This isn't a crime, just – the inevitable consequence of people who run out of – whose limitations . . .

PRIOR. Bang bang bang.
    The court will come to order.

LOUIS. I mean let's talk practicalities, schedules; I'll come over if you want, spend nights with you when I can, I can . . .

PRIOR. Has the jury reached a verdict?

LOUIS. I'm doing the best I can.

PRIOR. Pathetic. Who cares?

JOE. My whole life has conspired to bring me to this place, and I can't despise my whole life. I think I believed when I met you I could save you, you at least if not myself, but . . .
    I don't have any sexual feelings for you, Harper. And I don't think I ever did.

HARPER. I think you should go.

JOE. Where?

HARPER. Washington. Doesn't matter.

JOE. What are you talking about?

HARPER. Without me.
    Without me, Joe. Isn't that what you want to hear?

    *Little pause.*

JOE. Yes.

LOUIS. You can love someone and fail them. You can love someone and not be able to . . .

PRIOR. You *can*, theoretically, yes. A person can, maybe an editorial 'you' can love, Louis, but not *you*, specifically you, I don't know, I think you are excluded from that general category.

HARPER. You were going to save me, but the whole time you were spinning a lie. I just don't understand that.

PRIOR. A person could theoretically love and maybe many do but we both know now you can't.

LOUIS. I do.

PRIOR. You can't even say it.

LOUIS. I love you, Prior.

PRIOR. I repeat. Who cares?

HARPER. This is so scary, I want this to stop, to go back . . .

PRIOR. We have reached a verdict, your honour. This man's heart is deficient. He loves, but his love is worth nothing.

JOE. Harper . . .

HARPER. Mr Lies, I want to get away from here. Far away. Right now. Before he starts talking again. Please, please . . .

JOE. As long as I've known you Harper you've been afraid of . . . of men hiding under the bed, men hiding under the sofa, men with knives.

PRIOR. I'm dying! You stupid fuck! Do you know what that is! Love! Do you know what love means? We lived together four and a half years, you animal, you idiot.

LOUIS. I have to find some way to save myself.

JOE. Who are these men? I never understood it. Now I know.

HARPER. What?

JOE. It's me.

HARPER. It is?

PRIOR. GET OUT OF MY ROOM!

JOE. I'm the man with the knives.

HARPER. You are?

PRIOR. If I could get up now I'd kill you. I would. Go away. Go away or I'll scream.

HARPER. Oh God . . .

JOE. I'm sorry . . .

HARPER. It is you.

LOUIS. Please don't scream.

PRIOR. Go.

JOE. I tried to hide the knives but they're too sharp, and now they're cutting me open.

HARPER. I recognise you now.

LOUIS. Please . . .

JOE. Oh. Wait, I . . . Oh!
(*He covers his mouth with his hand, gags, and removes his hand, red with blood.*)
I'm bleeding.

PRIOR *screams*.

HARPER. Mr Lies.

MR LIES (*appearing, dressed in Antarctic exploration apparel*). Right here.

HARPER. I want to go away. I can't see him anymore.

MR LIES. Where?

HARPER. Anywhere. Far away.

MR LIES. Absolutamento.

HARPER *and* MR LIES *vanish*. JOE *looks up, sees that she's gone*.

PRIOR (*closing his eyes*). When I open my eyes you'll be gone.

LOUIS *leaves*.

JOE. Harper?

PRIOR (*opening his eyes*). Huh. It worked.

JOE (*calling*). Harper?

PRIOR. I hurt all over. I wish I was dead.

**Scene Ten**

HANNAH *and* SISTER ELLA CHAPTER, *a real estate*
*saleswoman,* HANNAH PITT's *closest friend, in front of* HANNAH's
*house in Salt Lake City.*

SISTER ELLA CHAPTER. Look at that view! A view of heaven.
Like the living city of heaven, isn't it, it just fairly glimmers in
the sun.

HANNAH. Glimmers.

SISTER ELLA CHAPTER. Even the stone and brick it just
glimmers and glitters like heaven in the sunshine. Such a nice
view you get, perched up on a canyon rim. Some kind of
beautiful place.

HANNAH. It's just Salt Lake, and it's hot, and you're selling the
house *for* me, not *to* me.

SISTER ELLA CHAPTER. I like to work up an enthusiasm for
my properties.

HANNAH. Just get me a good price.

SISTER ELLA CHAPTER. Well, the market's off.

HANNAH. At least fifty.

SISTER ELLA CHAPTER. Forty'd be more like it.

HANNAH. Fifty.

SISTER ELLA CHAPTER. Wish you'd wait a bit.

HANNAH. Well I can't.

SISTER ELLA CHAPTER. Wish you would. You're about the
only friend I got.

HANNAH. Oh well now.

SISTER ELLA CHAPTER. Know why I decided to like you? I
decided to like you 'cause you're the only unfriendly Mormon I
ever met.

HANNAH. Your wig is crooked.

SISTER ELLA CHAPTER. Fix it.

HANNAH *straightens* SISTER ELLA's *wig.*

SISTER ELLA CHAPTER. New York City. All they got there is
tiny rooms.

I always thought: people ought to stay put. That's why I got
my licence to sell real estate. It's a way of saying: Have a house!
Stay put! It's a way of saying travelling's no good. Plus I
needed the cash.

*She takes out a pack of cigarettes from her purse, lights one, offers pack
to* HANNAH.

HANNAH. Not out here, anyone could come by.

Nothing that came out of this house ever worked right
anyway. I won't be sorry to leave.

Oh, my life. God . . . hasn't spared me much.

It's a hard place, Salt Lake: baked dry. Abundant energy; not
much intelligence. That's a combination that can wear a body
out.

No harm looking someplace else. I don't need much room.

My sister-in-law Libby thinks there's radon gas in the
basement.

SISTER ELLA CHAPTER. Is there gas in the . . .

HANNAH. Of course not. Libby's a fool.

SISTER ELLA CHAPTER. 'Cause I'd have to include that in the
description.

HANNAH. There's no gas, Ella. (*Little pause.*) Give a puff.

HANNAH *takes furtive drag of* ELLA's *cigarette.*

HANNAH. Put it away now.

SISTER ELLA CHAPTER. So I guess it's goodbye.

HANNAH. You'll be alright, Ella, I wasn't ever much of a friend.

SISTER ELLA CHAPTER. I'll say something but don't laugh,
OK?

This is the home of saints, the godliest place on earth, they
say, and I think they're right. That mean there's no evil here?
No. Evil's everywhere. Sin's everywhere. But this . . . is the
spring of sweet water in the desert, the desert flower. Every
step a Believer takes away from here is a step fraught with
peril. I fear for you, Hannah Pitt, because you are my friend.
Stay put. This is the right home of saints.

HANNAH. Latter day saints.

SISTER ELLA CHAPTER. Only kind left.

HANNAH. But still. Late in the day . . . for saints and everyone. That's all. That's all.

Fifty thousand dollars for the house, Sister Ella Chapter; don't undersell. It's an impressive view.

## ACT THREE: NOT-YET-CONSCIOUS, FORWARD DAWNING     Late Winter 1985–86

### Scene One

*The stage is completely dark.* PRIOR *is having a nightmare. He wakes up, sits up in bed, and switches on a nightlight. He looks at his clock. Seated by the table near the bed is a man dressed in the clothing of a 13th-century British squire.*

PRIOR. Who are you?

PRIOR 1. My name is Prior Walter.

*Pause.*

PRIOR. My name is Prior Walter.

PRIOR 1. I know that.

PRIOR. Explain.

PRIOR 1. You're alive. I'm not. We have the same name. What do you want me to explain?

PRIOR. A ghost?

PRIOR 1. An ancestor.

PRIOR. Not *the* Prior Walter? The Bayeux Tapestry Prior Walter?

PRIOR 1. His great-great grandson. The fifth of the name.

PRIOR. I'm the thirty-fourth, I think.

PRIOR 1. Actually the thirty-second.

PRIOR. Not according to Mother.

PRIOR 1. She's including the two bastards, then; I say leave them out. I say no room for bastards. The little things you swallow . . .

PRIOR. Pills.

PRIOR 1. Pills. For the pestilence. I too . . .

PRIOR. Pestilence . . . You too what?

PRIOR 1. The pestilence in my time was much worse than now. Whole villages of empty houses. You could look outdoors and see Death walking in the morning, dew dampening the ragged hem of his black robe. Plain as I see you now.

PRIOR. You died of the plague.

PRIOR 1. The spotty monster. Like you, alone.

PRIOR. I'm not alone.

PRIOR 1. You have no wife, no children.

PRIOR. I'm gay.

PRIOR 1. So? Be gay, dance in your altogether for all I care, what's that to do with not having children?

PRIOR. Gay homosexual, not bonny, blithe and . . . never mind.

PRIOR 1. I had twelve. When I died. And I was three years older than you.
    The messenger come. Prepare the way. The infinite descent, the breath in air . . . It's an honour. Pity you have no sons to share it with.

*He vanishes.*

*Blackout.*


**Scene Two**

*The following night. Again the nightmare, PRIOR wakes up, this time to confront the PRIOR from the night before and also a new ghost, this one dressed in the clothing of an elegant 18th-century Londoner.*

PRIOR 1. Nightmares.

PRIOR 2. He should take one of his . . . um . . .

PRIOR 1. *Pills.*

PRIOR 2. Yes, *pills.* Your physick.

PRIOR. Oh God another one.

PRIOR 2. Prior Walter. Prior to you by some seventeen others.

PRIOR 1. He's counting the bastards.

PRIOR. Are we having a convention?

PRIOR 2. We beg pardon for the intrusion.

PRIOR 1. I don't.

PRIOR 2. Well no, I suppose . . .

PRIOR 1. I intrude nowhere, he's my descendant, he could welcome me better. Intrude . . .

PRIOR 2. We've been sent to declare her fabulous incipience. They love a well-paved entrance with lots of heralds, and . . .

PRIOR 1. The messenger come. Prepare.

PRIOR 2. They chose us, I suspect, because of the mortal affinities. In a family as long-descended as the Walters there are bound to be a few carried off by plague.

PRIOR 1. The spotty monster.

PRIOR 2. Black Jack. Came from a water pump, half the city of London, can you imagine? His came from fleas. Yours, I understand, is the lamentable consequence of venery . . .

PRIOR 1. Fleas on rats, but who knew that?

PRIOR. Am I going to die?

PRIOR 2. We aren't allowed to discuss . . .

PRIOR 1. When you do, you don't get ancestors to help you through it. You may be surrounded by children but you die alone.

PRIOR. I'm afraid.

PRIOR 1. You should be. There aren't even torches, and the path's rocky, dark and steep.

PRIOR 2. Don't alarm him. There's good news before there's bad. We two come to strew rose petal and palm leaf before the triumphal procession. Prophet. Seer. Revelator. It's a great honour for the family.

PRIOR 1. He hasn't got a family.

PRIOR 2. I meant for the Walters, for the family in the larger sense.

PRIOR (singing).

All I want is a room somewhere,
Far away from the cold night air . . .

PRIOR 2 (*putting a hand on* PRIOR's *forehead*). Calm, calm, this is
no brain fever . . .

PRIOR *calms down, but keeps his eyes closed. The lights begin to
change.*

| PRIOR 2. Even now, | PRIOR 1. (*low chant*). |
|---|---|
| From the mirror bright | Adonai, Adonai, |
|   halls of heaven, | Olam ha-yichud, |
| Across the cold and lifeless | Zefirot, Zazahot, |
|   infinity of space, | Ha-adam, ha-gadol |
| The Messenger comes | Daughter of Light, |
| Trailing orbs of light, | Daughter of Splendoura, |
| Fabulous, incipient, | Fluor! Phosphor! |
| Oh Prophet, | Lumen! Candle! |
| To you . . . | |

PRIOR 1 *and* PRIOR 2. Prepare, prepare,
The Infinite Descent,
A breath, a feather,
Glory to . . .

*They vanish.*

## Scene Three

*Split scene:* LOUIS *and* BELIZE *in a coffee shop.* PRIOR *is at the
outpatient clinic at the hospital with* EMILY, *the nurse; she has him on a
pentamidine IV drip.*

LOUIS. Why has democracy succeeded in America? Of course by
succeeded I mean comparatively, not literally, not in the
present, but what makes for the prospect of some sort of
radical democracy spreading outward and growing up? Why
does the power that was once so carefully preserved at the top
of the pyramid by the original framers of the constitution seem
drawn inexorably downward and outward in spite of the best
effort of the Right to stop this? I mean it's the really hard thing
about being Left in this country, the American Left can't help
but trip over all these petrified little fetishes: freedom, that's
the worst; you know, *Jeane Kirkpatrick* for God's sake will go on

and on about freedom and so what does that mean, the word
freedom, when she talks about it, or human rights; you have
Bush talking about human rights, and so what are these people
talking about, they might as well be talking about the mating
habits of Venusians, these people don't begin to know what,
ontologically, freedom is or human rights, like they see these
bourgeois property-based Rights-Of-Man-type rights but that's
not enfranchisement, not democracy, not what's implicit, what's
potential within the idea, not the idea with blood in it. That's
just liberalism, the worst kind of liberalism, really, bourgeois
tolerance, and what I think is that what AIDS shows us is the
limits of tolerance, that it's not enough to be tolerated, because
when the shit hits the fan you find out how much tolerance is
worth. Nothing. And underneath all the tolerance is intense,
passionate hatred.

BELIZE. Uh huh.

LOUIS. Well don't you think that's true?

BELIZE. Uh huh. It is.

LOUIS. *Power* is the object, not being tolerated. Fuck assimilation.
But I mean in spite of all this the thing about America, I think,
is that ultimately we're different from every other nation on
earth, in that, with people here of every race, we can't . . .
ultimately what defines us isn't race, but politics. Not like any
European country where there's an insurmountable fact of a
kind of racial, or ethnic, monopoly, or monolith, like all
Dutchmen, I mean Dutch people, are well, Dutch, and the Jews
of Europe were never Europeans, just a small problem. Facing
the monolith. But here there are so many small problems, it's
really just a collection of small problems, the monolith is
missing. Oh, I mean, of course I suppose there's the monolith
of White America. White Straight Male America.

BELIZE. Which is not unimpressive, even among monoliths.

LOUIS. Well, no, but when the race thing gets taken care of, and
I don't mean to minimalise how major it is, I mean I know it is,
this is a really, really incredibly racist country but it's like, well,
the British. I mean, all these blue-eyed pink people. And it's
just weird, you know, I mean I'm not all that Jewish-looking,
or . . . well, maybe I am but, you know, in New York, everyone
is . . . well, not everyone, but so many are but so but in
England, in London I walk into bars and I feel like Sid the Yid,

you know I mean like Woody Allen in *Annie Hall*, with the
payes and the gabardine coat, like never, never anywhere so
much – I mean, not actively despised, not like they're Germans,
who I think are still terribly anti-semitic, and racist too, I mean
black-racist, they pretend otherwise but, anyway, in London,
there's just . . . and at one point I met this black gay guy from
Jamaica who talked with a lilt but he said his family'd been
living in London since before the Civil War – the American one
– and how the English never let him forget for a minute that
he wasn't blue-eyed and pink and I said yeah, me too, these
people are anti-semites and he said yeah but the British Jews
have the clothing business all sewed up and blacks there can't
get a foothold. And it was an incredibly awkward moment of
just . . . I mean here we were, in this bar that was gay but it was
a *pub* you know, the beams and the plaster and those horrible
little, like, two-day-old fish and egg sandwiches – and just so
British, so *old*, and I felt, well, there's no way out of this
because both of us are, right now, too much immersed in this
history, hope is dissolved in the sheer age of this place, where
race is what counts and there's no real hope of change – it's the
racial destiny of the Brits that matters to them, not their
political destiny, whereas in America . . .

BELIZE. Here in America race doesn't count.

LOUIS. No, no, that's not . . . I mean you *can't* be hearing
that . . .

BELIZE. I . . .

LOUIS. It's – look, race, yes, but ultimately race here is a political
question, right? Racists just try to use race here as a tool in a
political struggle. It's not really about race. Like the spiritualists
try to use that stuff, are you enlightened, are you centred,
channelled, whatever, this reaching out for a spiritual past in a
country where no indigenous spirits exist – only the Indians, I
mean Native American spirits and we killed them off so now,
there are no gods here, no ghosts and spirits in America, there
are no angels in America, no spiritual past, no racial past,
there's only the political, and the decoys and the ploys to
manoeuvre around the inescapable battle of politics, the
shifting downwards and outwards of political power to the
people . . .

BELIZE. POWER to the People! AMEN! (*Looking at his watch.*)
*OH MY GOODNESS!* Will you look at the time, I gotta . . .

LOUIS. Do you . . . You think this is, what, racist or naive or something?

BELIZE. Well it's certainly *something*. Look, I just remembered I have an appointment . . .

LOUIS. What? I mean I really don't want to, like, speak from some position of privilege and . . .

BELIZE. I'm sitting here, thinking, eventually he's *got* to run out of steam, so I let you rattle on and on saying about maybe seven or eight things I find really offensive . . .

LOUIS. What?

BELIZE. But I know you, Louis, and I know the guilt fuelling this peculiar tirade is obviously already swollen bigger than your haemorrhoids . . .

LOUIS. I don't have haemorrhoids.

BELIZE. I hear different. May I finish?

LOUIS. Yes, but I don't have haemorrhoids.

BELIZE. So finally, when I . . .

LOUIS. Prior told you, he's an asshole, he shouldn't have . . .

BELIZE. You promised, Louis. Prior is not a subject.

LOUIS. You brought him up.

BELIZE. I brought up haemorrhoids.

LOUIS. So it's indirect. Passive-aggressive.

BELIZE. Unlike, I suppose, banging me over the head with your theory that America doesn't have a race problem.

LOUIS. Oh be fair I never said that.

BELIZE. Not exactly, but . . .

LOUIS. I said . . .

BELIZE. . . . but it was close enough, because if it'd been that blunt I'd've just walked out and . . .

LOUIS. You deliberately misinterpreted! I . . .

BELIZE. Stop interrupting! I haven't been able to . . .

LOUIS. Just let me . . .

BELIZE. NO! What, talk? You've been talking nonstop since I got here, yaddadda yaddadda blah blah blah, up the hill, down the hill, playing with your MONOLITH, and girlfriend it is truly an *awesome* spectacle but I got better things to do with my time than sit here listening to this racist bullshit just because I feel sorry for you that . . .

LOUIS. Well, you could have joined in at any time instead of . . .

LOUIS. I am not a racist!

BELIZE. Oh come on . . .

LOUIS. So maybe I am a racist but . . .

BELIZE. Oh I really hate that! It's no fun picking on you Louis; you're so guilty, it's like throwing darts at a glob of jello, there's no satisfying hits, just quivering, the darts just blop in and vanish.

LOUIS. I just think when you are discussing lines of oppression it gets very complicated and . . .

BELIZE. Oh is that a fact? You know, we black drag queens have a rather intimate knowledge of the complexity of the lines of . . .

LOUIS. *Ex*-black drag queen.

BELIZE. Actually ex-ex.

LOUIS. You're doing drag again?

BELIZE. I don't . . . Maybe. I don't have to tell you. Maybe.

LOUIS. I think it's sexist.

BELIZE. I didn't ask you.

LOUIS. Well it is. The gay community, I think, has to adopt the same attitude towards drag as black women have to take towards black women blues singers.

BELIZE. Oh my we *are* walking dangerous tonight . . .

LOUIS. Well, it's all internalised oppression, right, I mean the masochism, the stereotypes, the . . .

BELIZE. Louis, are you deliberately trying to make me hate you?

LOUIS. No, I . . .

BELIZE. I mean, are you deliberately transforming yourself into an arrogant, sexual-political Stalinist-slash-racist flag-waving thug for my benefit?

*Pause.*

LOUIS. You know what I think?

BELIZE. What?

LOUIS. You hate me because I'm a Jew.

BELIZE. I'm leaving.

LOUIS. It's true.

BELIZE. You have no basis except your . . .
    Louis, it's good to know you haven't changed; you are still an honorary citizen of the Twilight Zone, and after your pale, pale white polemics on behalf of racial insensitivity you have a flaming *fuck* of a lot of nerve calling me an anti-semite. Now I really gotta . . .

LOUIS. You called me Lou the Jew.

BELIZE. That was a joke.

LOUIS. I didn't think it was funny. It was hostile.

BELIZE. It was three years ago.

LOUIS. So?

BELIZE. You just called yourself Sid the Yid.

LOUIS. That's not the same thing.

BELIZE. Sid the Yid is different from Lou the Jew.

LOUIS. Yes.

BELIZE. Someday you'll have to explain that to me, but right now . . .
    *You* hate me because you hate black people.

LOUIS. I do not. But I do think most black people are anti-semitic.

BELIZE. 'Most black people'. That's racist, Louis, and *I* think most Jews . . .

LOUIS. Louis Farrakhan.

BELIZE. Ed Koch.

LOUIS. Jesse Jackson.

BELIZE. Jackson. Oh really, Louis, this is . . .

LOUIS. Hymietown! Hymietown!

BELIZE. Louis, you voted for Jesse Jackson. You send cheques to the Rainbow Coalition.

LOUIS. I'm ambivalent. The cheques bounced.

BELIZE. All your cheques bounce, Louis; you're ambivalent about everything.

LOUIS. What's that supposed to mean?

BELIZE. You may be dumber than shit but I refuse to believe you can't figure it out. Try.

LOUIS. I was never ambivalent about Prior. I love him. I do. I really do.

BELIZE. Nobody said different.

LOUIS. Love and ambivalence are . . . Real love isn't ambivalent.

BELIZE. 'Real love isn't ambivalent.' I'd swear that's a line from my favourite bestselling paperback novel, *In Love with the Night Mysterious*, except I don't think you ever read it.

*Pause.*

LOUIS. I never read it, no.

BELIZE. You ought to. Instead of spending the rest of your life trying to get through *Democracy in America*. It's about this white woman whose Daddy owns a plantation in the Deep South in the years before the Civil War – the American one – and her name is Margaret, and she's in love with her daddy's number one slave, and his name is Thaddeus, and she's married but her white slave-owner husband has AIDS: Antebellum Insufficiently Developed Sexorgans. And there's a lot of hot stuff going down when Margaret and Thaddeus can catch a spare torrid ten under the cotton-picking moon, and then of course the Yankees come, and they set the slaves free, and the slaves string up old Daddy, and so on. Historical fiction. Somewhere in there I recall Margaret and Thaddeus find the time to discuss the nature of love; her face is reflecting the flames of the burning plantation – you know, the way white people do – and his black face is dark in the night and she says to him, 'Thaddeus, real love isn't ever ambivalent.'

*Little pause.* EMILY *enters and turns off IV drip*

BELIZE. Thaddeus looks at her; he considers her thesis; and he isn't sure he agrees.

EMILY (*removing IV drip from* PRIOR*'s arm*). Treatment number . . . (*Consulting chart.*) Four.

PRIOR. Pharmaceutical miracle. Lazarus breathes again.

LOUIS. Is he . . . How bad is he?

BELIZE. You want the laundry list?

EMILY. Shirt off, let's check the . . .

PRIOR *takes his shirt off. She examines his lesions during:*

BELIZE. There's the weight problem and the shit problem and the morale problem.

EMILY. Only six. That's good. Pants.

*He drops his pants. He's naked. She examines.*

BELIZE. And. He thinks he's going crazy.

EMILY. Looking good. What else?

PRIOR. Ankles sore and swollen, but the leg's better. The nausea's mostly gone with the little orange pills. BM's pure liquid but not bloody anymore, for now, my eye doctor says everything's OK, for now, my dentist says 'Yuck!' when he sees my fuzzy tongue, and now he wears little condoms on his thumb and forefinger. And a mask. So what? My dermatologist is in Hawaii and my mother . . . well leave my mother out of it. Which is usually where my mother is, out of it. My glands are like walnuts, my weight's holding steady for week two, and a friend died two days ago of bird tuberculosis; bird tuberculosis; that scared me and I didn't go to the funeral today because he was an Irish Catholic and it's probably open casket and I'm afraid of . . . something, the bird tuberculosis or seeing him or . . . So I guess I'm doing OK. Except for of course I'm going nuts.

EMILY. We ran the toxoplasmosis series and there's no indication . . .

PRIOR. I know, I know, but I feel like something terrifying is on its way, you know, like a missile from outer space, and it's plummeting down towards the earth, and I'm ground zero, and . . . I am generally known where I am known as one cool, collected queen. And I am ruffled.

EMILY. There's really nothing to worry about. I think that shochen bamromim hamtzeh menucho nechono al kanfey haschino.

PRIOR. What?

EMILY. Everything's fine. Bemaalos k'doshim ut'horim kezohar horokeea mazhirim . . .

PRIOR. Oh I don't understand what you're . . .

EMILY. Es nishmas Prior sheholoch leolomoh, baavur shenodvoo z'dokoh b'ad hazkoras nishmosoh.

PRIOR. Why are you doing that! Stop it! Stop it!

EMILY. Stop what?

PRIOR. You were just . . . weren't you just speaking in Hebrew or something.

EMILY. *Hebrew*? (*Laughs.*) I'm basically Italian-American. No. I didn't speak in Hebrew.

PRIOR. Oh no, Oh God please I really think I . . .

EMILY. Look, I'm sorry, I have a waiting room full of . . . I think you're one of the lucky ones, you'll live for years, probably – you're pretty healthy for someone with no immune system. Are you seeing someone? Loneliness is a danger. A therapist?

PRIOR. No, I don't need to see anyone, I just . . .

EMILY. Well think about it. You aren't going crazy. You're just under a lot of stress. No wonder . . . (*She starts to write in his chart.*)

*Suddenly there is an astonishing blaze of light, a huge chord sounded by a gigantic choir, and a great book with steel pages mounted atop a molten-red pillar pops up from the stage floor. It opens; there is a large Aleph inscribed on its pages, which bursts into flames. Immediately the book slams shut and disappears instantly under the floor as the lights become normal again. EMILY notices none of this, writing. PRIOR is agog.*

EMILY (*laughing, exiting*). Hebrew . . .

LOUIS. Help me.

BELIZE. I beg your pardon?

LOUIS. You're a nurse, give me something, I . . . don't know
what to do anymore, I . . . Last week at work I screwed up the
Xerox machine like permanently and so I . . . then I tripped on
the subway steps and my glasses broke and I cut my forehead,
here, see, and now I can't see much and my forehead . . . it's
like the Mark of Cain, stupid, right, but it won't heal and every
morning I see it and I think, Biblical things, Mark of Cain,
Judas Iscariot and his silver and his noose, people who . . . in
betraying what they love betray what's truest in themselves, I
feel . . . nothing but cold for myself, just cold, and every night I
miss him, I miss him so much but then . . . those sores, and the
smell and . . . where I thought it was going . . . I could be . . . I
could be sick too, maybe I'm sick too. I don't know.
  Belize. Tell him I love him. Can you do that?

BELIZE. I've thought about it for a very long time, and I still
don't understand what love is. Justice is simple. Democracy is
simple. Those things are unambivalent. But love is very hard.
And it goes bad for you if you violate the hard law of love.

LOUIS. I'm dying.

BELIZE. He's dying. You just wish you were.
  Oh cheer up, Louis. Look at that heavy sky out there . . .

LOUIS. Purple.

BELIZE. *Purple*? Boy, what kind of a homosexual are you,
anyway? That's not purple, Mary, that colour up there is (*Very
grand.*) *mauve*.
  All day today it's felt like Thanksgiving. Soon, this . . .
ruination will be blanketed white. You can smell it – can you
smell it?

LOUIS. Smell what?

BELIZE. Softness, compliance, forgiveness, grace.

LOUIS. No . . .

BELIZE. I can't help you learn that. I can't help you, Louis.
You're not my business. (*He exits.*)

LOUIS *puts his head in his hands, inadvertently touching his cut forehead.*

LOUIS. Ow FUCK! (*He stands slowly, looks towards where* BELIZE *exited.*)

Smell what?

(*He looks both ways to be sure no one is watching, then inhales deeply, and is surprised.*) Huh. Snow.

**Scene Four**

HARPER *in a very white, cold place, with a brilliant blue sky above; a delicate snowfall. She is dressed, for warmth, in layers upon layers of mismatched clothing. The sound of the sea, faint.*

HARPER. Snow! Ice! Mountains of ice! Where am I? I . . .
I feel better, I do, I . . . feel better. There are ice crystals in my lungs, wonderful and sharp. And the snow smells like cold, crushed peaches. And there's something . . . some current of blood in the wind, how strange, it has that iron taste.

MR LIES. Ozone.

HARPER. Ozone! Wow! Where am I?

MR LIES. The Kingdom of Ice, the bottom-most part of the world.

HARPER (*looking around, then realising*). Antarctica. This is Antarctica!

MR LIES. Cold shelter for the shattered. No sorrow here, tears freeze.

HARPER. Antarctica, Antarctica, oh boy oh boy, LOOK at this, I . . . Wow, I must've really snapped the tether, huh?

MR LIES. Apparently . . .

HARPER. That's great. I want to stay here forever. Set up camp. Build things. Build a city, an enormous city made up of frontier forts, dark wood and green roofs and high gates made of pointed logs and bonfires burning on every street corner. I should build by a river. Where are the forests?

MR LIES. No timber here. Too cold. Ice, no trees.

HARPER. Oh details! I'm sick of details! I'll plant them and grow them. I'll live off caribou fat, I'll melt it over the bonfires and drink it from long, curved goat-horn cups. It'll be great. I want to make a new world here. So that I never have to go home again.

MR LIES. As long as it lasts. Ice has a way of melting . . .

HARPER. No. Forever. I can have anything I want here – maybe even companionship, someone who has . . . desire for me. You, maybe.

MR LIES. It's against the by-laws of the International Order of Travel Agents to get involved with clients. Rules are rules. Anyway, I'm not the one you really want.

HARPER. There isn't anyone . . . maybe an eskimo. Who could ice-fish for food. And help me build a nest for when the baby comes.

MR LIES. There are no eskimo in Antarctica. And you're not really pregnant. You made that up.

HARPER. Well all of this is made up. So if the snow feels cold I'm pregnant. Right? Here, I can be pregnant. And I can have any kind of a baby I want.

MR LIES. This is a retreat, a vacuum, its virtue is that it lacks everything; deep-freeze for feelings. You can be numb and safe here, that's what you came for. Respect the delicate ecology of your delusions.

HARPER. You mean like no eskimo in Antarctica.

MR LIES. Correcto. Ice and snow, no eskimo. Even hallucinations have laws.

HARPER. Well then who's that?

*The* ESKIMO *appears*.

MR LIES. An eskimo.

HARPER. An Antarctic eskimo. A fisher of the polar deep.

MR LIES. There's something wrong with this picture.

*The* ESKIMO *beckons*.

HARPER. I'm going to like this place. It's my own National

Geographic Special! Oh! Oh! (*She holds her stomach.*) I think . . .
I think I felt her kicking. Maybe I'll give birth to a baby
covered with thick white fur, and that way she won't be cold.
My breasts will be full of hot cocoa so she doesn't get chilly.
And if it gets really cold, she'll have a pouch I can crawl into.
Like a marsupial. We'll mend together. That's what we'll do;
we'll mend.

**Scene Five**

*An abandoned lot in the South Bronx. A homeless woman is standing
near an oil drum in which a fire is burning. Snowfall. Trash around.
HANNAH enters dragging two heavy suitcases.*

HANNAH. Excuse me? I said excuse me? Can you tell me where
I am? Is this Brooklyn? Do you know a Pineapple Street? Is
there some sort of bus or train or . . .?
    I'm lost, I just arrived from Salt Lake. City. Utah? I took the
bus that I was told to take and I got off – well it was the very
last stop, so I had to get off, and I *asked* the driver was this
Brooklyn, and he nodded yes but he was from one of those
foreign countries where they think it's good manners to nod at
everything even if you have no idea what it is you're nodding
at, and in truth I think he spoke no English at all, which I
think would make him ineligible for employment on public
transportation. The public being English-speaking, mostly. Do
you speak English?

*The woman nods.*

HANNAH. I was supposed to be met at the airport by my son.
He didn't show and I don't wait more than three and three-
quarters hours for *anyone*. I should have been patient, I guess,
I . . . Is this . . .

WOMAN. Bronx.

HANNAH. Is that . . . The *Bronx*? Well how in the name of
Heaven did I get to the Bronx when the bus driver said . . .

WOMAN (*talking to herself*). Slurp slurp slurp will you STOP that
disgusting slurping! YOU DISGUSTING SLURPING
FEEDING ANIMALS Feeding yourself, just feeding yourself,
what would it matter, to you or to ANYONE, if you just
stopped. Feeding. And DIED?

*Pause.*

HANNAH. Can you just tell me where I . . .

WOMAN. Why was the Koskiosko Bridge named after a Polack?

HANNAH. I don't know what you're . . .

WOMAN. That was a joke.

HANNAH. Well what's the punchline?

WOMAN. I don't know.

HANNAH. Oh for pete's sake, is there anyone else who . . . (*She looks around.*) No one anywhere.

WOMAN (*again, to herself*). Stand further off you fat loathsome whore, you can't have anymore of this soup, slurp slurp slurp you animal, and the – I know you'll just go pee it all away and where will you do that? Behind what bush? It's FUCKING COLD out here and I . . .
Oh that's right, because it was supposed to have been a tunnel! That's not very funny.
Have you read the prophecies of Nostradamus?

HANNAH. Who?

WOMAN. Some guy I went out with once somewhere, Nostradamus. Prophet, outcast, eyes like . . . Scary shit, he . . .

HANNAH. Shut up. Please. Now I want you to stop jabbering for a minute and pull your wits together and tell me how to get to Brooklyn. Because you know! And you are going to tell me! Because there is no one else around to tell me and I am wet and cold and I am very angry! So I am sorry you're psychotic but just make the effort – take a deep breath – DO IT!

HANNAH *and the* WOMAN *breathe together.*

HANNAH. That's good. Now exhale.

*They do.*

HANNAH. Good. Now how do I get to Brooklyn?

WOMAN. Don't know. Never been. Sorry. Want some soup?

HANNAH. Manhattan? Maybe you know . . . I don't suppose you know the location of the Mormon Visitor's . . .

WOMAN. 65th and Broadway.

HANNAH. How do you . . .

WOMAN. Go there all the time. Free movies. Boring, but you can stay all day.

HANNAH. Well . . . So how do I . . .

WOMAN. Take the D Train. Next block make a right.

HANNAH. Thank you.

WOMAN. Oh yeah. In the new century I think we will all be insane.

### Scene Six

JOE and ROY. ROY *has made a considerable effort to look well. He isn't well, and he hasn't succeeded much in looking it.*

JOE. I can't. The answer's no. I'm sorry.

ROY. Oh, well, apologies . . .
I can't see that there's anyone asking for apologies.

*Pause.*

JOE. I'm sorry, Roy.

ROY. Oh, well, apologies.

JOE. My wife is missing, Roy. My mother's coming from Salt Lake to . . . to help look, I guess. I'm supposed to be at the airport now, picking her up but . . . I just spent two days in a hospital, Roy, with a bleeding ulcer, I was spitting up blood.

ROY. Blood, huh? Look, I'm very busy here and . . .

JOE. It's just a job.

ROY. A job? A *job*? *Washington*! Dumb Utah Mormon hick shit!

JOE. Roy . . .

ROY. WASHINGTON! When Washington called me I was younger than you, you think I said 'Aw fuck no I can't go I got two fingers up my asshole and a little moral nosebleed to boot!' When Washington calls you, my pretty young punk friend, you go or you can go fuck yourself sideways 'cause the train has pulled out of the station, and you are *out*, nowhere, out in the cold. Fuck you, Mary Jane, get outta here.

JOE. Just let me . . .

ROY. Explain? Ephemera. You broke my heart. Explain that.
Explain that.

JOE. I love you. Roy.
  There's so much that I want, to be . . . what you see in me, I
want to be a participant in the world, in your world, Roy, I
want to be capable of that, I've tried, really I have but . . . I
can't do this. Not because I don't believe in you, but because I
believe in you so much, in what you stand for, at heart, the
order, the decency. I would give anything to protect you,
but . . . There are laws I can't break. It's too ingrained. It's not
me. There's enough damage I've already done.
Maybe you were right, maybe I'm dead.

ROY. You're not dead, boy, you're a sissy.
  You love me; that's moving, I'm moved. It's nice to be loved.
  I warned you about her, didn't I, Joe? But you don't listen to
me, why, because you say Roy is smart and Roy's a friend but
Roy . . . well, he isn't nice, and you wanna be nice. Right? A
nice, nice man!

*Little pause.*

You know what my greatest accomplishment was, Joe, in my
life, what I am able to look back on and be proudest of? And I
have helped make Presidents and unmake them and mayors
and more goddam judges than anyone in NYC ever – AND
several million dollars, tax-free – and what do you think means
the most to me?
You ever hear of Ethel Rosenberg? Huh, Joe, huh?

JOE. Well, yeah, I guess I . . . Yes.

ROY. Yes. Yes. You have heard of Ethel Rosenberg. Yes. Maybe
you even read about her in the history books.
  If it wasn't for me, Joe, Ethel Rosenberg would be alive
today, writing some personal advice column for *Ms.* magazine.
She isn't. Because during the trial, Joe, I was on the phone
every day, talking with the judge . . .

JOE. Roy . . .

ROY. Every day, doing what I do best, talking on the telephone,
making sure that timid Yid nebbish on the bench did his duty
to America, to history. That sweet unprepossessing woman, two
kids, boo-hoo-hoo, reminded us all of our little Jewish mamas –

she came this close to getting life; I pleaded till I wept to put her in the chair. Me. I did that. I would have fucking pulled the switch if they'd have let me. Why? Because I fucking hate traitors. Because I fucking hate communists. Was it legal? Fuck legal. Am I a nice man? Fuck nice. They say terrible things about me in *The Nation*. Fuck *The Nation*. You want to be Nice, or you want to be Effective? Make the law, or be subject to it. Choose. Your wife chose. A week from today, she'll be back. SHE knows how to get what SHE wants. Maybe I ought to send *her* to Washington.

JOE. I don't believe you.

ROY. Gospel.

JOE. You can't possibly mean what you're saying.
Roy, you were the Assistant District Attorney on that case, ex parte communication with the judge during the trial would be . . . censurable, at least, probably conspiracy and . . . in a case that resulted in execution, it's . . .

ROY. What? Murder.

JOE. You're not well is all.

ROY. What do you mean, not well? Who's not well?

*Pause.*

JOE. You said . . .

ROY. No I didn't. I said what?

JOE. Roy, you have cancer.

ROY. No I don't.

*Pause.*

JOE. You told me you were dying.

ROY. What the fuck are you talking about, Joe? I never said that. I'm in perfect health. There's not a goddam thing wrong with me.

ROY *smiles.*

Shake?

JOE *hesitates. He holds out his hand to* ROY. Roy *pulls* JOE *to him in a strong clench.*

ROY (*more to himself than to* JOE). It's OK that you hurt me because I love you, baby Joe. That's why I'm so rough on you.

ROY *releases* JOE.

ROY. Prodigal son. The world will wipe its dirty hands all over you.

JOE. It already has, Roy.

ROY. Now go.

ROY *shoves* JOE, *hard.* JOE *starts to leave.* ROY *stops him.*

ROY. (*smoothing* JOE's *lapels, tenderly*). I'll always be here, waiting for you . . .
(*Then again, with sudden violence, pulling* JOE *close.*)
What did you want from me, what was all this, what do you want, treacherous ungrateful little . . .

JOE, *very close to belting* ROY, *grabs him by the front of his robe, and propels him across the length of the room.*

ROY (*softly, delighted*). Transgress a little, Joseph. There are so many laws; find one you can break.

JOE *lets go. Hesitates, and then leaves.* ROY *doubles over in great pain, which he's been hiding throughout the scene with* JOE.

ROY. Ah, Christ . . .
Andy! Andy! Get in here! Andy!

*The door opens, but it isn't* ANDY. *A small Jewish woman dressed modestly in a fifties hat and coat enters the room. The room darkens.*

ROY. Who the fuck are you? The new nurse?

*The figure in the doorway says nothing. She stares at* ROY. *A pause.* ROY *looks at her carefully, gets up, crosses to her.* ROY *crosses back to the chair, sits heavily.*

ROY. Aw, fuck. Ethel.

ETHEL ROSENBERG. You don't look good, Roy.

ROY. Well, Ethel. I don't feel good.

ETHEL ROSENBERG. But you lost a lot of weight. That suits you. You were heavy back then. Zaftig, mit hips.

ROY. I haven't been that heavy since 1960. We were all heavier back then, before the body thing started. Now I look like a skeleton. They stare.

ETHEL ROSENBERG. The shit's really hit the fan, huh, Roy?

ROY *nods.*

ETHEL ROSENBERG. Well, don't expect me to feel too sorry.

ROY. What is this, Ethel, hallowe'en? You trying to scare me?

ETHEL *says nothing*.

ROY. Well you're wasting your time! I'm scarier than you any day of the week! So beat it, Ethel! BOOO! BETTER DEAD THEN RED! Somebody trying to shake me up? HAH HAH! From the throne of God in heaven to the belly of hell, you can all fuck yourselves and then go jump in the lake because I'M NOT AFRAID OF YOU OR DEATH OR HELL OR ANYTHING!

ETHEL ROSENBERG (*starting to leave*). Be seeing you soon, Roy. Julius sends his regards.

ROY. Yeah, well send this to Julius!

*He flips the bird in her direction, stands and moves towards her, intending to slam the door in her face. Halfway across the room he slumps to floor, breathing laboriously, in pain.*

ETHEL ROSENBERG. You're a very sick man, Roy.

ROY. Oh God . . . ANDY!

ETHEL ROSENBERG. Hmmm. He doesn't hear you, I guess. We should call the ambulance.

*She goes to the phone.*

    Hah! Buttons! Such things they got now.
    What do I dial, Roy?

*Pause. ROY looks at her, then:*

ROY. 911.

ETHEL ROSENBERG. (*dials the phone*). It sings!
(*Imitating dial tones.*) La la la . . .
    Huh.

    Yes, you should please send an ambulance to the home of Mister Roy Cohn, the famous lawyer.
    What's the address, Roy?

ROY. 244 East 87th.

ETHEL ROSENBERG. 244 East 87th Street. No apartment number, he's got the whole building. Me? An old friend.

*She hangs up.*

They said a minute.

ROY. I have all the time in the world.

ETHEL ROSENBERG. You're immortal.

ROY. I'm immortal. I have *forced* my way . . . into history, Ethel. I ain't never gonna die.

ETHEL ROSENBERG (*a dry little laugh, then*). History . . . is about to crack wide open, Millennium approaches.


## Scene Seven

PRIOR's *bedroom.* PRIOR 1 *watching* PRIOR *in bed, who is staring back at him, terrified. Tonight* PRIOR 1 *is dressed in weird alchemical robes and hat over his historical clothing, and he carries a long palm leaf bundle.*

PRIOR 1. Tonight's the night! Aren't you excited? Tonight she arrives!
Right through the roof! Ha-adam, Ha-gadol . . .

PRIOR 2 (*appearing, similarly attired*). Lumen! Phosphor! Fluor! Candle! An unending billowing of scarlet and . . .

PRIOR. Look. Garlic. A mirror. Holy Water. A crucifix. FUCK OFF! Get the fuck out of my room! GO!

PRIOR 1 (*to* PRIOR 2). Hard as a hickory knob, I'll bet.

PRIOR 2. We all tumesce when they approach. We wax full, like moons.

PRIOR 1. Dance.

PRIOR. Dance?

PRIOR 1. Stand up, dammit, give us your hands, dance!

PRIOR 2. Listen . . .

*A lone oboe begins to play a little dance tune.*

PRIOR 2. Delightful sound. Care to dance?

PRIOR. Please leave me alone, please just let me sleep . . .

PRIOR 2. Ah, he wants someone familiar. A partner who knows his steps. (*To* PRIOR.) Close your eyes. Imagine . . .

PRIOR. I don't . . .

PRIOR 2. Hush. Close your eyes.

  PRIOR *does.*

PRIOR 2. Now open them.

  PRIOR *does.* LOUIS *appears. He looks gorgeous. The music builds a little into a full-blooded waltz.*

PRIOR. Lou.

LOUIS. Dance with me.

PRIOR. I can't, my leg, it hurts at night . . .
    Are you . . . a ghost, Lou?

LOUIS. No. Just spectral. Lost to my self. Sitting all day on cold park benches. Wishing I could be with you. Dance with me, babe . . .

  PRIOR *stands up. They begin to dance. The music is beautiful.*

PRIOR 1 (*to* PRIOR 2). Hah. Now I see why he's got no children. He's a sodomite.

PRIOR 2. Oh be quiet, you medieval gnome, and let them dance.

PRIOR 1. I'm not interfering, I've done my bit. Hooray, hooray, the messenger's come, now I'm blowing off. I don't like it here.

  PRIOR 1 *vanishes.*

PRIOR 2. The twentieth century. Oh dear, the world has gotten so terribly, terribly old.

  PRIOR 2 *vanishes.* LOUIS *and* PRIOR *waltz happily. Lights fade back to normal.* LOUIS *vanishes.* PRIOR *dances alone. Then suddenly, the sound of wings fills the room.*


**Scene Eight**

PRIOR *alone in his apartment.*
LOUIS *alone in the park.*
*Again, a sound of beating wings.*


PRIOR. Oh don't come in here don't come in . . . LOUIS!!
    No. My name is Prior Walter, I am . . . the scion of an

ancient line, I am . . . abandoned I . . . no, my name is . . . is . . .
Prior and I live . . . here and now, and . . . in the dark, the
Recording Angel opens its hundred eyes and snaps the spine of
the Book of Life and . . . hush! Hush!
    I'm talking nonsense, I . . .
    No more mad scene, hush, hush . . .

LOUIS *in the park on a bench.* JOE *approaches, stands at a distance.
They stare at each other, then* LOUIS *turns away.*

LOUIS. Do you know the story of Lazarus?

JOE. Lazarus?

LOUIS. Lazarus. I can't remember what happens, exactly.

JOE. I don't . . . Well, he was dead, Lazarus, and Jesus breathed
life into him. He brought him back from death.

LOUIS. Come here often?

JOE. No. Yes. Yes.

LOUIS. Back from the dead. You believe that really happened?

JOE. I don't know anymore what I believe.

LOUIS. This is quite a coincidence. Us meeting.

JOE. I followed you.
    From work. I . . . followed you here.

*Pause.*

LOUIS. You followed me.
    You probably saw me that day in the washroom and thought:
there's a sweet guy, sensitive, cries for friends in trouble.

JOE. Yes.

LOUIS. You thought maybe I'll cry for you.

JOE. Yes.

LOUIS. Well I fooled you. Crocodile tears. Nothing . . . (*He
touches his heart, shrugs.*)

JOE *reaches tentatively to touch* LOUIS's *face.*

LOUIS (*pulling back*). What are you doing? Don't do that.

JOE (*withdrawing his hand*). Sorry. I'm sorry.

LOUIS. I'm . . . just not . . . I think, if you touch me, your hand might fall off or something. Worse things have happened to people who have touched me.

JOE. Please.
  Oh, boy . . .
  Can I . . .
  I . . . want . . . to touch you. Can I please just touch you . . . um, here?

  JOE *puts his hand on one side of* LOU's *face. He holds it there.*

JOE. I'm going to hell for doing this.

LOUIS. Big deal. You think it could be any worse than New York City?

  LOUIS *puts his hand on* JOE's *hand. He takes* JOE's *hand away from his face, holds it for a moment, then kisses it.*

LOUIS. Come on.

JOE. Where?

LOUIS. Home. With me.

JOE. This makes no sense. I mean I don't know you.

LOUIS. Likewise.

JOE. And what you do know about me you don't like.

LOUIS. The Republican stuff?

JOE. Yeah, well for starters.

LOUIS. I don't not like that. I *hate* that.

JOE. So why on earth should we . . .

  LOUIS *goes to* JOE *and kisses him.*

LOUIS. Strange bedfellows. I don't know. I never made it with one of the damned before.
  I would really rather not have to spend tonight alone.

JOE. I'm a pretty terrible person, Louis.

LOUIS. Lou.

JOE. No, I really really am. I don't think I deserve being loved.

LOUIS. There? See? We already have a lot in common.

  LOUIS *stands, begins to walk away. He turns, looks back at* JOE. JOE *follows. They exit.*

PRIOR *listens. At first no sound, then once again, the sound of beating wings, frighteningly near.*

PRIOR. That sound, that sound, it . . . What is that, like birds or something, like a *really* big bird, I'm frightened, I . . . no, no, fear, find the anger, find the . . . anger, my blood is clean, my brain is fine, I can handle pressure, I am a gay man and I am used to pressure, to trouble, I am tough and strong and . . . Oh. Oh my goodness. I . . . (*Looks down at his crotch. He is washed over by an intense sexual feeling.*) Ooohhhh . . . I'm hot, I'm . . . so . . . aw Jeez what is going on here I . . . must have a fever I . . . OH! PLEASE, OH PLEASE! Something's coming in here, I'm scared, I don't like this at all, something's approaching and I . . . OH!

*There is a creaking and a groaning from the bedroom ceiling, which rains plaster dust. The bedside light flickers wildly. Then there is a great blaze of triumphal music, heralding. The light turns an extraordinary harsh, cold, pale blue, then a rich, brilliant warm golden colour, then a hot, bilious green, and then finally a spectacular royal purple.*

PRIOR (*an awestruck whisper*). God almighty . . .
Very Steven Spielberg.

*A sound, like a plummeting meteor, tears down from very, very far above the earth, hurtling at an incredible velocity towards the bedroom; the light seems to be sucked out of the room as the projectile approaches; as the room reaches darkness, we hear a terrifying CRASH as something immense strikes earth; the whole building shudders and a part of the bedroom ceiling, lots of plaster and lathe and wiring, crashes to the floor. And then in a shower of unearthly white light, spreading great opalescent grey-silver wings, the angel descends into the room and floats above the bed.*

ANGEL. Greetings, Prophet;
    The Great Work begins:
    The Messenger has arrived.

**Blackout.**

**End of Part One.**